Cambridge Elements

Elements in Histories of Emotions and the Senses
edited by

AFFECTIVE TOUCHING

Neurobiology and Technological Applications

Mark Paterson
University of Pittsburgh

Shaftesbury Road, Cambridge CB2 8EA, United Kingdom

One Liberty Plaza, 20th Floor, New York, NY 10006, USA

477 Williamstown Road, Port Melbourne, VIC 3207, Australia

314–321, 3rd Floor, Plot 3, Splendor Forum, Jasola District Centre, New Delhi – 110025, India

103 Penang Road, #05–06/07, Visioncrest Commercial, Singapore 238467

Cambridge University Press is part of Cambridge University Press & Assessment, a department of the University of Cambridge.

We share the University's mission to contribute to society through the pursuit of education, learning and research at the highest international levels of excellence.

www.cambridge.org
Information on this title: www.cambridge.org/9781009484367

DOI: 10.1017/9781009484404

When citing this work, please include a reference to the DOI 10.1017/9781009484404

First published 2025

A catalogue record for this publication is available from the British Library

ISBN 978-1-009-48436-7 Hardback
ISBN 978-1-009-48437-4 Paperback
ISSN 2632-1068 (online)
ISSN 2632-105X (print)

Affective Touching

Neurobiology and Technological Applications

Elements in Histories of Emotions and the Senses

DOI: 10.1017/9781009484404
First published online: February 2025

Mark Paterson
University of Pittsburgh

Author for correspondence: Mark Paterson, paterson@pitt.edu

Abstract: At the end of the twentieth century the discovery of 'slow', affective touch nerves in humans known as C-tactile (CT) afferents, which are entirely separate from the faster pathways for touching objects, had huge social implications. The Swedish neuroscientists responsible formulated an "affective touch hypothesis" or "social touch hypothesis" to consider their purpose. Section 1 offers a history of the science of social touch, from related discoveries in mammals by physiologists in the 1930s, to the recent rediscoveries of the CT nerves in humans. Section 2 considers how these findings are being intentionally folded into technologies for interaction: first, as mediated social touch, communicating at a distance through haptics and second, with the increasing number of social and service robots in healthcare and domestic settings, the role of affective touch within human–robot interaction design.

This Element also has a video abstract: www.cambridge.org/HOES-Paterson

Keywords: touch, affect, social touch, haptics, robotics

ISBNs: 9781009484367 (HB), 9781009484374 (PB), 9781009484404 (OC)
ISSNs: 2632-1068 (online), 2632-105X (print)

Contents

Introduction

Why do slow tactile behaviours, such as hugging and stroking, feel good and enhance social bonds? The significance of these behaviours has long been observed in academic areas such as social psychology and nonverbal communication studies. Yet the impressively large literature on the senses, including psychology and neuroscience, has tended to ignore these forms of touch. The neurophysiological explanations behind slow touching in humans have only emerged at the cusp of the twenty-first century and are beginning to spread beyond the immediate neuroscientific community into other areas of research. What is less widely known is that the foundations for what some neuroscientists are calling 'social' or 'affective' touch were established in the early twentieth century with pioneering physiologists Otfrid Foerster in Germany and, a few years later, Yngwe Zotterman in Sweden. One of the purposes of this Element is to resurface some of this research from the archives, delving into some detail from their animal studies and others' human studies, the better to contextualize the celebrated breakthroughs in the neuroscience of human touching in recent decades.

Using techniques that he pioneered, Zotterman discovered 'slow' or unmyelinated (i.e. without a fatty sheath that aids conductivity) nerves in mammals, predominantly cats, that provided sensations of tickling, burning, itching and warmth that differed from the usual understanding of 'fast' touch with myelinated (sheathed), thin Aβ fibres. Instead, Zotterman recorded responses from what are now termed C-fibre low-threshold mechanoreceptors (CLTMs), known in humans as C-tactile (CT) afferents. Strangely, Foerster and then Zotterman's pioneering research seemed to be virtually neglected in the wider academic world until the 1990s. The presence of C-tactile (CT) afferents in humans was presumed to have disappeared through evolutionary processes until their extensive presence in humans was confirmed using microneurographic techniques in Sweden, first by Roland Johansson in Umeå (Johansson et al., 1988) and then by Magnus Nordin in Uppsala, both conducting research on human facial nerves (Nordin, 1990). But the true implications of these discoveries only began to be realized in a pioneering paper by Åke Vallbo, Håkan Olausson, Johan Wessberg and Ulf Norsell in Gothenburg a few years later (Vallbo et al., 1993). It was this small team of Swedish researchers in Gothenburg who grasped the real import of C-tactile (CT) afferents activated by the slow stroking of particular hairy skin areas in mammals and then humans. The rediscovery, which broke through into mainstream science reporting at the time, prompted fascinating questions. Why had this crucial aspect of touch and the investigation of CT afferents been 'forgotten' for five decades? What is their actual function, and what are these other aspects of touch *for*, exactly? In the first short paper on the topic by the Gothenburg team, Vallbo et al. put this in an understated way: 'Their biological role remains an enigma which might attract more attention now that their existence in man has been demonstrated' (1993, p. 301). The gateway for thinking about the social and emotional role of this separate, newly rediscovered nerve pathway in humans and mammals had suddenly opened wide, and all manner of speculation and hypothesis about the social aspects could rush in.

Over the past three decades the Gothenburg team has collaborated widely and produced a large number of studies extending this research. Increasingly, some of this research has speculated on significant social implications of the production of pleasurable bonding sensations between participants, which led to the release of hormones including oxytocin. The neurophysiological explanation has been called the 'affective touch hypothesis' by some scientists (Olausson et al., 2010), or the 'social touch hypothesis' by others (e.g. India Morrison 2016a, 2016b, 2023). A paper in *Nature Neuroscience* (Olausson et al., 2002) which emerged out of this research was instrumental in publicizing this new area of research, as it was this paper that became widely reported in the media. For example, when interviewed by BBC News, Olausson explained: 'We have discovered a new sensory system in man that transmits information about touch with a slow speed to the brain. This slow touch system does not signal what we mean by touch in daily life. Instead it signals the pleasant aspects that can be evoked by touch stimulation' (BBC, 2002).

However, a central difficulty remains. Much of the speculation surrounding the 'social' in social touch is being done by neuroscientists, and recent scholarship in the social sciences and humanities has failed to take account of these separate tactile pathways. This short Element can only begin to address these problems over two related sections. First, by offering a brief history of the relatively recent neuroscience of social touch, explaining the discovery of these parallel and complementary pathways to a readership perhaps unfamiliar with the scientific literature. Why did it take so long for it to become scientifically identified and experimentally verified? What are some of the wider social implications for this new neurophysiology of touch? Second, by considering current and near-future implementations through sociotechnical imaginaries and future haptic technologies. How might these recently discovered experimental findings help us implement touch through technologies so that it can be reproduced and felt over a distance or through machines? What is *mediated social touch*, and how does it relate to this neuroscientific story?

This Element is structured to address such questions in as straightforward a manner as possible, with the intention of imposing some order for those unfamiliar with the manifold loops, circuits, pathways, reflexes, and relays of the nervous system between the centre and periphery of the body. It consists of two sections, dealing with the history of social touch in Section 1, ‘A Brief History of the Science of Social Touch’, and then the futures of social touch in Section 2, ‘Social Touch and Its Mediations: Socio-technological Applications’. Each section is subdivided into subsections. Section 1 navigates through a number of classic but also less widely known scientific studies to lay out a narrative about the rediscovery of affective forms of touching in the scientific laboratory. In 1.1, I identify how one set of circuits of the mammalian nervous system, followed by studies with humans, has become scientifically entrenched from the early nineteenth century onwards as *discriminative* touch, that is, cutaneous (skin-based) touch which prompts the consciousness of spatial and durational contact (Paterson, 2007, 2021). The discovery in the early twentieth century of slow, unmyelinated nerve fibres that detect other forms of touching by Otfrid Foerster and then Yngwe Zotterman therefore opens a gateway to more socially complex forms of touching. Section 1.2, ‘Rediscovering Earlier Nerve Pathways’, therefore shows how the neurocartography of touch becomes modified towards the end of the twentieth century with discoveries in Sweden by Vallbo, Olausson and others of a separate, complementary nervous circuit that deals with *affective*, rather than *discriminatory*, touch. So far, both sections are partially constrained by the emphasis on individual neurophysiology. As Boddice and Smith argue in the first Element in this series, there is a risk for even social neuroscience that it privilege the ‘internal’, that is, ‘what happens inside the brain and body, how things work, how sensations and emotions are produced or, to be more correct, *constructed*’, as opposed to the more socially complex ‘biocultural brain-body’ (Boddice & Smith, 2020, p. 35). Hence in 1.3, ‘Social Touch in the Wild’, and then the entirety of Section 2, I branch out to explore some wider implications of the ‘affective touch hypothesis’ or ‘social touch hypothesis’. The purpose of Section 2 is to pose questions about the futures of social touch, asking how some of the neurophysiological circuits and loops identified in Section 1 might be transposed or integrated into more complex social touching behaviours effected through technology. This is achieved through two analogues of haptic communication, first the ‘handshake’ and then the ‘hug’. In 2.1 what has recently coalesced into the phrase ‘Mediated Social Touch’ (e.g. Haans & Ijsselsteijn, 2006, 2009; Huisman, 2012) works as an umbrella term for a range of technologies through which we may communicate affective or social touch over a distance, and so implications for the future of telepresence and online communication are considered. This amounts to, and is exemplified by, the story of a transatlantic ‘virtual handshake’ between two PHANToM haptic devices. Finally, in 2.2 the issue of touch in human–robot interaction (HRI) is addressed, as more social and healthcare robots enter our lives. A brief survey of social robots that invite tactile interaction then culminates in a very literal 'robot hug' with the HuggieBot project, designed specifically to promote social touch. Meanwhile, elsewhere in HRI there is increasingly a confluence of technologies which might produce what Dumouchel and Damiano (2017), Asada (2014, 2015a, 2015b), and others term 'Artificial Empathy', or AE, something that will complement the rise of AI. This section therefore builds on the observations of social touch 'in the wild' in 1.3 to underline how haptics is a highly effective yet currently underutilized communicative channel between humans and robots.

Some Background to the World of Touch

Before embarking on historical aspects of the neuroscience of touch, it might be fruitful to take a step back to explain some terminology around haptics, touch and related senses. Along with sight and hearing, touch is actively explored in a variety of scientific and engineering fields, including psychology, neuroscience and human-machine interfaces. Nevertheless, in popular understanding touch is often reduced to the mechanics and sensations of skin pressure (mechanoreception) alone, which could be received passively as stimuli. Touch is active, exploratory, sometimes involving the recognition and manipulation of objects through the hands. It therefore comprises other related forms of sensation, including sensitivity to temperature (thermoreception), pain (nociception), bodily position in space (proprioception) and the sense of movement of the body or limbs (kinaesthesia) (see e.g. Paterson, 2007, 2009, 2021). Rather than think of touch as a single sense, then, psychologist James J. Gibson referred to the 'haptic system' as a perceptual cluster which informs the organism of its immediate environment. In his classic work of ecological psychology, *The Senses Considered as Perceptual Systems*, Gibson distinguishes the haptic system from the usual understanding of touch as skin pressure:

> The haptic system, then, is an apparatus by which the individual gets information about both the environment and his body. He feels an object relative to the body and the body relative to an object. It is the perceptual system by which animals and men are *literally* in touch with the environment. (Gibson, 1968, p. 97, original emphasis)

The concept of haptics in engineering and robotics, meanwhile, tends to be centred on the production of systems that reproduce realistic-seeming sensations for users to actively touch and interact with objects, as we explore further in Section 2. Founder of the International Society for Haptics, Engineer Gabriel Robles-De-La-Torre has worked extensively with touch in computer interfaces and in Virtual Environments. Touch and its related senses, he argues, are 'critical for normal human functioning at many different levels, from controlling the body to perceiving the environment, as well as learning about and interacting with it' (2006, p. 29). However, haptics in this world of engineering applications is less expansive than Gibson's human 'haptic system'. Gibson had explicitly distinguished between the everyday understandings of touch and the psychology of the haptic system. 'It is not just the sense of skin pressure', Gibson argued. 'It is not even the sense of pressure plus the sense of kinesthesis' (1968, p. 97). Yet the majority of haptics engineers are indeed focussing on the role of cutaneous sensation and kinesthesis in facilitating active manipulation of objects. As Robles-De-La-Torre puts it:

> In experimental psychology and physiology, the word 'haptic' refers to the ability to experience the environment through active exploration, typically with our hands, as when palpating an object to gauge its shape and material properties. This is commonly called active or haptic touch, in which cutaneous and kinesthetic capabilities have important roles. (Robles-De-La-Torre, 2006, p. 27)

In other words, the form of touch most commonly considered in the public understanding is cutaneous touch, the sensation of pressure on the skin. The forms of touch that are reproduced through electromechanical means are most commonly cutaneous touch combined with kinesthesis, the sense of movement of body or limbs, all in order to aid the recognition and manipulation of objects. These forms of touch are discriminative; that is, they rely on certain nerve pathways. Not the C-tactile afferents that were rediscovered but rather Aβ low threshold mechanoreceptors and Aδ fibres for pain and temperature (see e.g. McGlone et al., 2014, p. 738). These pathways allow the boundaries between subject and object to be perceived, or in the vein of Gibson's haptic system, an organism to be 'in touch with' its environment. What about other forms of touch, affective or social touch, in which the subject is not simply determining or distinguishing itself from its physical environment but inextricably involved in a social environment with others?

1 A Brief History of the Science of Social Touch

1.1 Mapping the Neurophysiology of 'Inner' and 'Outer' Touch

Historically, scientific work on the measurement of the body's response to touch ignored affective responses, and instead sought to objectively measure touch and pain sensations over areas of the experimental subject's skin, effectively to 'map' tactile sensitivity and thresholds of sensation (see also Fretwell, 2020; Parisi, 2018; Paterson, 2019, 2021). This is obviously not the place for an exhaustive history of the development of the psychology and neurophysiology of touch. However, it is worth highlighting a few other areas of touch research to better grasp the scientific landscape in the nineteenth and early twentieth centuries, ahead of the more detailed account of the discovery of C-tactile (CT) nerve fibres and their role in social touch. Research on the measurement of discriminative touch response was first developed in laboratories in Leipzig by Ernst Heinrich Weber in the 1830s and 1840s with his book *De Tactu* ['On touch'] of 1834, and then *Der Tastsinn und Gemeingefühl* ['The sense of touch and common sensibility'] in 1846 (Weber, 1996). Weber was measuring thresholds of response on the skin of predominantly male subjects within the laboratory through instruments such as the *Stangenzirkel* ('beam compass'), von Frey hairs and the aesthesiometer. The standard aesthesiometer, invented by Edward Sieveking in 1858, is a handheld metal ruler with a pair of points, one of which can be moved along and fixed to precise distances from the end point, the better to measure two-point tactile discrimination on the skin. More sensitive skin areas are able to detect shorter distances between two points, and vice versa. Von Frey hairs (or filaments) are a set of specially calibrated natural fibres attached to a wooden handle that could exert a consistent force on the skin before buckling, a device invented by Maximillian Von Frey in 1896 and still in use in various forms today, like the earlier psychophysics experiments on pain and touch performed by Charles Verdin in Paris and Joseph Jastrow at Johns Hopkins (see e.g. Paterson, 2021, pp. 216–218). The *Stangenzirkel* or beam compass is like a set of wooden compasses with points at the end of each arm, with a calibrated ruler between them to measure precise distance. This scientific project was the isolation and subsequent standardized measurement of sensation that could be compared across populations, an objective measure based on the subject's reported sensations (the so-called JND, or 'just noticeable difference', as a unit of measurement). For Weber in *Der Tastsinn* ['The sense of touch', 1834], such experiments could not determine whether the nerves responsible for detecting pressure were also involved in temperature, pain or itching. '*It is therefore still uncertain, whether those structures responsible for sensations of pressure are the same as the ones that transmit sensations of warmth and cold, or whether there is a structure which is specialized to transmit these sensations*' (Weber, 1996, p. 202, original emphasis).

Weber's research was followed decades later by the 'godfather of psychophysics' Gustav Fechner, who, in *Elements of Psychophysics* (Fechner, 1860), also concentrated on discriminative pathways, and this mapping exercise was designed to produce a normative psychoanatomical model of tactile and pain responses, with the pioneering early criminologist Cesare Lombroso using the aesthesiometer instead to map pathological responses and therefore identify potential for deviance and criminality in *L'uomo delinquente* ['Criminal man']

(Lombroso, 1876). Conducting measurements with a desk-bound aesthesiometer, for example, Lombroso found a comparative lack of tactile sensitivity in female prostitutes and male criminals. The early twentieth century brought pioneering neurophysiologists in Britain like Charles Sherrington and Edgar Adrian, the latter who collaborated with Yngwe Zotterman in Sweden on discerning nerve fibres responsible for touch, itch, and pain, as discussed in substantial detail in Section 1.1.2. But around this time David Katz's *Der Aufbau der Tastwelt* [The World of Touch] of 1925 is notable. In addition to the quantitative measurement of skin deformation, reaction time and the influence of vibration and temperature on touch in his laboratory studies, Katz also offered a more phenomenological analysis of touch that prefigures Maurice Merleau-Ponty's discussion of the role of touch and the spatiality of the body in *Phénoménologie de la perception* of 1945 (Merleau-Ponty, 2013), by considering the role of one's own body as a tactual object, for example, and regarding 'movement as fundamentally an elementary formative factor in actual phenomena, as well-nigh as indispensable for touch as light is for colour sensations' (Katz, 1989, p. 76).

The role of movement in active touching and manipulation, and the shift from skin surface to sensations of the bodily interior that Katz considers, leads to another related 'tangent' of touch research, differentiating forms of 'inner' sensations felt within the body from the concentration on cutaneous touch. This started off as rather loose, a jumble of imprecise inner touch and movement sensations, including what Ebbinghaus (1902), who had encountered Fechner's work on psychophysics in Paris, had termed *eigenartige Empfindungen* (strange sensations), or Wilhelm Wundt (1896, p. 134) had formulated as *innere Tastempfindungen* ('inner touch sensations', as distinguished from *äußerer* or 'outer' touch). Some of these ideas were translated and somewhat popularized in the Anglophone world as 'organic sensations' by E. B. Titchener (1908). Such inner forms of touch involved other somatosensory information such as pain and itch, the stretch receptors in muscle spindles, fatigue and the feeling of muscular effort, the sense of movement and so on (for more detail see Paterson, 2021, pp. 27–83; 2023a). What some German physiologists including George, Schäfer and Goldscheider termed the 'muscle sense' or *Muskelsinn* around 1870 had currency for a while until the term fell out of favour around 1900. The vagueness of hypothetical ideas about 'inner touch' from the late nineteenth century came to become more precisely defined and measured as the cartography of the human nervous system progressed. David Howes for example makes the claim that 'the anatomical basis of the doctrine of the inner senses was discredited by advances in physiology' (2009, p. 20). Hence a growing consensus emerged among Anglophone physiologists in the 1870s such as

David Ferrier and George Henry Lewes to reject any idea of a distinct 'muscle sense'. William James' essay 'The Feeling of Effort' of 1880, and the second volume of *Principles of Psychology* (1890), explicitly dismissed any putative 'muscle sense' as being 'vague'.

Out of this vagueness of inner senses and organic sensations, the more physiologically precise concepts of 'kinaesthesia' and then 'proprioception' emerge. The former is coined by neurologist and physiologist Henry Charlton Bastian (1869). Kinaesthesia is a compound noun that adds movement (*kinein*) to the Greek root *aisthêsis* (feeling), together constituting a sense or feeling of movement. The latter, 'proprioception', first coined by Charles Sherrington (1906), was derived from *proprius*, the sense of one's own body. Not only did these terms offer greater physiological credence to what had previously been vaguely defined muscular sensations but also there was now differentiation between actual touching and the subjectively felt sensations of movement and position. For example, Bastian in his 1869 essay 'On the Muscular Sense, and on the Physiology of Thinking' proffers the idea of a *kinaesthetic* rather than muscular sense that can still be differentiated from discriminative touch on the skin: 'there is evidence to show that the brain is assisted in the execution of voluntary movements by guiding impressions of some kind', but that these impressions were distinct from the 'ordinary cutaneous' sensations or of 'deep sensibility' (Bastian, 1869, p. 463).

1.1.1 Charles Sherrington: Interoception, Proprioception, and the Reflex System

Charles Scott Sherrington at Oxford was one of the pioneers of the physiological investigation of the sensory nervous system and awarded the Nobel Prize for Physiology or Medicine in 1932 with Edgar Adrian (later Lord Adrian) for their efforts. Sherrington provides a direct route both conceptually and physiologically between the sensory nerves of the muscles, the spinal cord (spinothalamic tract) and the region within the cerebrum known as the motor cortex. Through a series of papers, and documented in notes and letters in the Wellcome Trust archives and elsewhere (see Paterson, 2021), he was trying to map the pathway of peripheral sensory and motor nerves through the spinal cord, and to further differentiate the processes of 'interoception' from touch and other senses. As opposed to the externally oriented or what he termed 'extero-ceptive' senses like vision and smell, he suggested 'intero-ception' (Sherrington, 1907). This term remains in use in neuroscience, such as in the work of American neuroscientist A. D. 'Bud' Craig, who used fMRI imaging to map the perception of the inner state of the body through an 'interoceptive cortex' which includes 'the cortical representations of several highly resolved, distinct sensations, including temperature, pain, itch, muscular and visceral sensations, sensual touch and other feelings from the body' (Craig, 2003, p. 660). Sherrington's research led to a wider and more encompassing theory of integrated reflex circuits within the organism, as explored in his 1906 book *The Integrative Action of the Nervous System*. In that book, and a subsequent 1907 paper, he first defined 'proprioception', where receptors positioned throughout the muscular tissues and accessory organs (tendons, joints, blood vessels) provide feedback to the organism on its posture, position and movement (Sherrington, 1906, pp. 129–130).

The 'integrated' aspect of the nervous system is significant. Based on experimental surgical data, he envisioned an integrated bodily whole based on nested loops of primitive and then more complex reflexes. The reflex was an elementary or fundamental unit, regarded by Herbert Spencer for example as 'the atom of the psyche' (in Jeannerod, 1985, p. 44). The reflex arc was the most basic element of the nervous system insofar as its function could be integrated and coordinated through the cerebral cortex. Simple reflexes are adjusted into an ordered 'reflex pattern', thought Sherrington, and there must be orderly changes from one reflex pattern to another, a 'co-ordination of reflexes successively proceeding' (Sherrington 1906, p. 8) from one to the other within the organism, and ultimately between the organism and its immediate environment. He extended the work of Kühne on the muscle spindle, identifying sensory fibres within the muscle tissue that provide feedback directly to the spinal cord for tonus (muscle position) and posture, proving definitively that muscle is in fact a sensory organ. Sherrington had built upon the work of Marshall Hall and Johannes Müller to more systematically develop the idea of this 'reflex arc', a way that sensory stimulus and motor response remains localized, operating between a part of the body and the spinal cord without having to relay centrally to the cerebellum (and back). By not being transported the full extent of the nerve trunk, up through the spinal cord and into the brain regions, the speed of transmission inward to the spinal cord through sensory nerves (afferent pathways) and outward through motor nerves (efferent pathways) to effect muscular activity, is far faster. Sherrington had observed behaviours in the laboratory which suggested this arc was present even within primitive organisms. Yet what intrigued him was how the complexity of the many potential reflex pathways, what he sometimes calls 'segments' or even 'metameres' in the case of organisms like the earthworm (1906, p. 314), somehow effected an overall 'functional unity', an oft-repeated phrase in the book (e.g., 1906, pp. 77–79, 314), within the organism as a whole. An organism's receptor organs initiate the reflex reactions in the nerve centres of each segment or metamere, and fall into two categories with different associated fields: the 'deep' or proprioceptive field, and the surface field, comprising exteroceptive and interoceptive regions. An organism's capacity for exteroception, the arrangement of receptors for the perception of external stimuli such as touch and pain, leads to a far richer 'extero-receptive field' than that of 'intero-ception' (Sherrington, 1906, p. 316ff). Whereas the 'intero-ceptive field' is associated with the visceral or the alimentary, and the 'extero-receptive field' is predominantly cutaneous (Sherrington, 1906, p. 320), the third, 'proprio-ceptive field' Sherrington associates with depth rather than surface.

In the psychophysics laboratory, what was measured and inscribed was the discriminatory particulars of cutaneous touch for the human subject, where sensitivity to stimulation of mechanoreceptors on the skin surface was reported vocally in terms of spatial location and duration (where, how long). For Sherrington, a different diagram of the nervous system was being produced, one comprised of receptive fields (RF), and a system of reflexes and reflex arcs which started to map out both afferent and efferent nervous pathways between the bodily periphery, via the spinal column, to their cerebral terminus; Sherrington thought this terminus was the Rolandic Fissure (now known as the central sulcus) which lies between the primary somatosensory (S1) and primary motor cortices. We will now update and complicate that picture.

1.1.2 Otfrid Foerster and Yngwe Zotterman: Mapping C Fibres for Other Forms of Touch

The idea that a particular brain area was responsible for the movement of the body was first postulated by the British neurologist John Hughlings Jackson in 1864 (York & Steinberg, 2011, p. 3107). Over time, this idea became focussed into a 'motor cortex', a region of the cerebral cortex dedicated to the planning, control and execution of voluntary movements. Its existence was experimentally verified over subsequent decades by David Ferrier in England, and Fritsch and Hitzig in Berlin (see e.g. Paterson, 2021, p. 27ff). Otfrid Foerster in Breslau started to map the motor cortex in 1932 through invasive neurosurgical experimentation (Foerster, 1936), and the neurosurgical mapping would continue with the American-born Canadian neurosurgeon Wilder Penfield, who visited Foerster before returning to Canada and establishing the Montreal Neurological Institute in 1934. With his assistant Oskar Gagel in Breslau, Foerster identified an association between the spinal cord and affective touch in their wide-ranging paper that can be translated as 'The anterior cord transection in man: A clinical-patho-physiological-anatomical study' (Foerster & Gagel, 1932). The study involved carefully severing the anterior (front) portion of the spinal cord, with the expectation that major and irreversible nerve damage would ensue. Foerster and Gagel's study revealed important evidence of a pathway through which not just pain but also temperature information was transmitted. This pathway is now termed the spinothalamic tract, part of the anterolateral system, known to be a major pathway in the nervous system responsible for transmitting sensory information. McGlone, Wessberg and Olausson credit Foerster with the earliest observation that 'cutting this tract impacts on aspects of affective touch (as well as pain and itch)' (McGlone et al., 2014, p. 742). For Foerster and Gagel, these findings were significant and part of a raft of other sensory effects:

> In addition to the sensation of pain and temperature, other sensory qualities are also affected by the transection of the anterior cord, especially the feeling of tickling and itching, and in general all feelings of pleasure or pain. The tickling sensation that normally occurs when stroking the hair is completely absent in the skin areas affected by the transection of the anterior cord; *There is only a naked sensation of touch.* (Foerster & Gagel, 1932, p. 43; author's translation, emphasis added)

One of the patients in this study was a tobacconist who had severe gastric problems, so they performed a transection of both the anterior and lateral tracts. The man 'stated that since the operation he had no libido, no feeling of sensual pleasure during cohabitation', and was unable to orgasm. 'The sexual act has become a purely sensory process for him', wrote Foerster and Gagel (1932, p. 43; author's translation).

As McGlone, Weissberg and Olausson argue, the lack of 'pleasure' after severance of the anterior side of the spinothalamic tract suggests that C-tactile (CT) afferents ascend in the same tract as the pain-bearing C-nociceptors. This was borne out later by evidence from cordotomy, that is, the surgical procedure of cutting through spinal cord fibres in order to reduce chronic intractable pain, which is a similar procedure to anterolateral transection. Like the subjects in Foerster and Gagel, who experience no strong pleasure or pain, patients who have undergone cordotomy report that 'they do not experience cutaneous erotic sensation when receiving low-intensity tactile stimulation' (2014, p. 742). As a result, this confirms Foerster and Gagel's much earlier evidence that the spinothalamic tract includes CT-afferents as well as C-nociceptor fibres.

A few years after Foerster and his team's experiments in Germany, in Sweden physiologist Yngwe Zotterman published results from his experiments at the Karolinska Institutet, a medical research facility in Stockholm. As he recounts in a career retrospective only three years before he died, his early research was stimulated by reading a series of papers by Edgar Adrian and Keith Lucas at Cambridge on the nervous system of frogs. Adrian and Lucas' experiments on the sciatic nerve of the frog were mapping muscle twitches as an indication of what occurs in motor nerve fibres. Zotterman went to Cambridge to work with Adrian for a short time in 1920, and then again in 1925 with funding from the Rockefeller Foundation, specifically to work on recording the electrical response of sensory nerves. Adrian had been using a capillary electrometer, which measures differences in electric current. Now Adrian 'wanted to go further and see what was signalled in single sensory nerve fibers', starting this project in October 1925 (Zotterman, 1979, p. 6). The place of such muscular nerves in the control of movement had been pioneered by Sherrington in Oxford (Sherrington, 1907) (see Paterson, 2021, p. 27ff). Adrian had been told, incorrectly it turns out, that the sternocutaneous muscle in the frog's chest terminated in a single muscle spindle, this being the ideal nerve to isolate and record. They worked feverishly, but Zotterman found that the muscle spindle consisted of multiple nerves. After much effort he managed to separate out a single afferent nerve fibre and record electrical responses by means of an electrometer, and recorded it through photography. Zotterman wrote decades later that 2 November 1925 was significant, a 'red letter day':

> Adrian ran in and out controlling the recording apparatus in the dark-room and developing the photographic plates. We were excited, both of us quite aware that what we now saw had never been observed before and that we were discovering a great secret of life, how the sensory nerves transmit their information to the brain . . . [T]he principal idea about the sensory nerves, the relation between the strength of stimulation and nervous response, we conceived that very day. (Zotterman, 1979, pp. 7–8)

What they called 'axone potential' is in modern parlance the action potential, that is, the electrical signals that propagate along the length of the sensory or motor nerve fibre. What Adrian and Zotterman achieved in 1925 had never been done before, to directly record both the strength of the stimulation and the speed and strength of nervous response. A year later they tried to work on cats, first the optical nerve although without success, and then the plantar nerve. They published 'The impulses produced by sensory nerve endings' (Adrian & Zotterman, 1926) based on data recorded from the peripheral nerves of cats signalling proprioception, touch (mechanoreception, at this time) and pain (nociception).

In 1927 Zotterman had returned to Sweden but continued his research on the role of sensory afferents in cats, constructing a capillary electrometer to better record the impulses of individual sensory nerves. In this early research, Zotterman was working on isolating sensory fibres that happened to be myelinated, in Schirmer et al.'s words 'because of their large and evident response to stimulation' (2023, p. 2). Zotterman had isolated an extremely thin fibre from the cat's plantar nerve, and for months was attempting to measure responses with the new equipment. Despite applying intense heat, and unlike other nerves he had isolated and recorded, the nerve's response was unexpectedly minimal. This remained puzzling for him throughout 1927–28 (Zotterman, 1979). The mystery was solved at the International Congress of Physiology in Boston in 1929, where Herbert Spencer Gasser and Joseph Erlanger gave the first demonstration of action potentials of thinner unmyelinated nerve fibres of very slow conduction. These were Class C fibres, or C afferents, under their own classification system, and their research was published in a paper of 1930, 'The action potential in fibers of slow conduction in spinal roots and somatic nerves' (Erlanger & Gasser, 1930).

As the 1930s progressed, Zotterman was exploring the role of touch and its relationship to pain (sharp pain and burning pain), itching, tickling and temperature in the cat's nervous system. His paper of 1936 for example measured potentials in the lingual nerve in the tongue of the cat, which consisted of a bundle of fine fibres of between 0.1 and 0.05 mm, only one of which he found was specifically responsible for detecting cold temperatures (Zotterman, 1936). His experiments involved dropping water of various temperatures onto the cat's tongue, including hot water to burn it, directly measuring pain and temperature sensations. This measurement was achieved by use of the electrometer, where action potentials of the nerves were amplified and then output visually through a cathode-ray oscillograph (CRO, or oscilloscope), a double-ray electron oscillograph for his later studies of 1939, and, in some cases, also outputting as sound through a loudspeaker. His 1937 paper 'A note on the relation between conduction rate and fibre size in mammalian nerves' continued his cat studies but involved the cutaneous nerves in the skin. Both here and in his previous paper, based on his experiments with frogs and then with cats, he confirms earlier studies by for example Gasser and Erlanger in 1927 and Blair and Erlanger in 1933, that showed that the recorded spike heights (i.e. the peaks of action potential across the nerve recorded by the electrometer) varied according to the square of the diameter (Zotterman, 1937, p. 125). Zotterman showed that this tracks from frogs (phalangeal nerve terminating in the feet) to cats (saphenous nerve in the leg).

In 1939 Zotterman published two related papers on the neurophysiology of touch and associated sensations in cats which discussed the role of types of afferent nerves and their relative 'axone potential', distinguishing between what were then termed β (beta), δ (delta) and C fibres under the now generally accepted Erlanger-Gasser classification (Erlanger & Gasser, 1930). The first two are classified as Group A (myelinated) nerves, Aβ and Aδ, respectively, whereas the last is from the unmyelinated Group C nerves, one of which would later be labelled the C-tactile or CT nerve. His paper for *Acta Psychiatrica Scandinavica*, 'The nervous mechanism of touch and pain' (Zotterman, 1939a), examined measured potentials for touch and pain, whereas his article for *Journal of Physiology*, 'Touch, pain and tickling: An electro-physiological investigation on cutaneous sensory nerves' (Zotterman, 1939b), examined the measured potentials with the same equipment, but this time with reference to itching and tickling as well. Incidentally, although the graphs produced by the electrometer and cathode ray oscillograph were straightforwardly reproducible in printed papers, for these studies the amplifier also fed into a loudspeaker to provide an aural representation: 'When the electrical response is lead [*sic*] to a loudspeaker . . . the C potentials due to their slow rate of conduction are heard as distant kettle-drums, which are easily distinguished from the higher pitch given by the more rapidly conducted potentials (β and δ)' (Zotterman, 1939a, p. 94). Certainly, among the noise of signals from all nerve fibres, having a clearly differentiable audio guide to the nerve signals would be an additional benefit.

In both papers Zotterman alludes to the familiar phenomenon that different types of touching produce different sensations, and this also varies according to which skin areas are touched. Light stroking versus continual pressing, for example, or hairy forearm compared with hairless palm. However, the fact that '*quantitative* changes in the strength of a mechanical stimulus produce very definite *qualitative* changes in the sensation', as he puts it, indicates that these different sensations must 'depend upon different nerve mechanisms' (Zotterman, 1939b, p. 5, my emphasis). While in the previous century Weber was measuring human subjects' responses to touch but was unable to explain the mechanisms behind this, Zotterman, as indicated by the titles of his papers, was attempting to distinguish underlying neurophysiological differences between touch and other cutaneous sensations such as sharp pain, dull pain, temperature, itching and tickling, all of which might seem phenomenologically related yet are underpinned by distinct and separate nervous mechanisms. Morrison (2016a, p. 9) explains that data about the properties of different nerve fibres were able to be gathered through the pioneering techniques of neurophysiologists including Zotterman in the first half of the twentieth century through electroneurograms, placing electrodes directly into bundles of peripheral nerve fibres in the flesh to measure the electrical current, plotted as a graph. Each nerve type has different firing properties in terms of latency, magnitude and habituation of responses to stimulation, and so the different nerve types can be discerned through these corresponding patterns. Zotterman continues:

> Thus the sensations that are generally spoken of as touch cannot be due to a simple mechanism, but must be of a heterogeneous nature. The sensations experienced from the palm of the hand when a finger-tip is pressing on it are of a quite different character from the tickling and faintly itching sensation experienced when the finger-tip passes very gently over the skin. (Zotterman, 1939b, p. 5)

His experiments showed that pain, specifically the type of 'burning pain', 'must be mediated by very thin nerve fibres of very slow conduction' such as C fibres (1939a, p. 91), whereas the sharp pain resulting from insertion of a needle relied on faster transmission initially through β fibres, followed by a 'massive' response by δ_1 and δ_2 fibres, and then 'an after-discharge consistently of C potentials' (Zotterman, 1939a, p. 94). In both papers published in 1939 he included the same diagram (see Figure 1) with axes showing diameter of fibres versus speed of conduction, indicating the significance and role of the C fibres in his studies. This study on pain involved experimentation on cats again in order to investigate axon potentials in sensory nerves, but this time Zotterman used the leg rather than the tongue, referring to 'slender branches of the saphenous nerve of the cat when pulling or twisting the hairs of its skin' (Zotterman, 1939a, p. 91). Adding to observations of his earlier research about the relation between

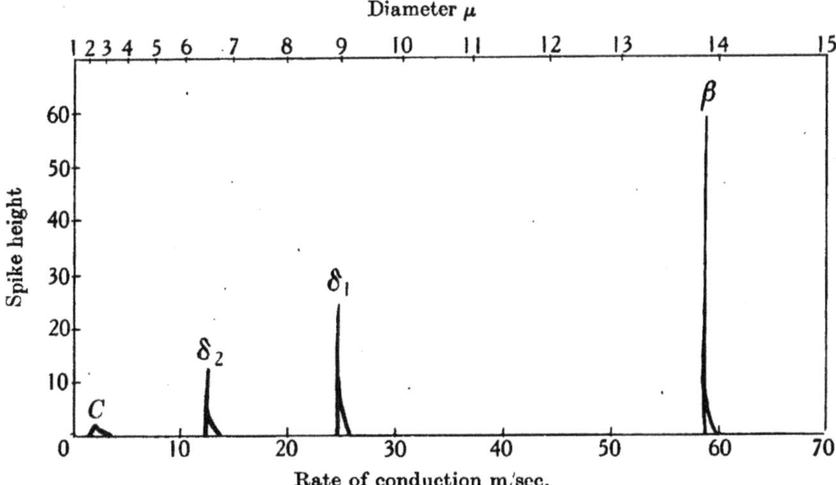

Figure 1 Diagram from Zotterman (1939b) showing relation between spike height of potentials reached in the axons, rate of conduction and diameter of the nerve fibre. The rate of conduction increases from 'thin and slow' unmyelinated C afferents (on left) to 'fat and fast' myelinated beta afferents (on right). Reproduced from *The Journal of Physiology*, Copyright John Wiley and Sons, with permission.

amplitude of action potential and the diameter of the nerve fibre (Zotterman, 1937), he summarized that 'fibres mediating cold, heat and burning pain from the tongue are of smaller dimensions than the largest fibres responding to touch and pressure' (Zotterman, 1939a, p. 92). For sharp pain, such as that induced by a needle, the profile of the action potentials across the fibres is similar to that of burning pain, with β fibres firing followed by δ_1 and δ_2 fibres, and an 'after-discharge consisting chiefly of C potentials follows', he writes. Although both 1939 papers involve similar data and observations, the biophysical difference between the fibres is mentioned in each only in passing, the fact that some fibres are myelinated and others not: 'The δ fibres are most probably myelinated fibres responsible for the "first pain sensation", while some C potentials at least seem to be unmyelinated fibres in the sense that their sheaths are not stained by osmic acid', he writes (Zotterman, 1939a, p. 95). Just as with the types of pain, in the case of tickling and itching, based on measured action potentials, Zotterman claimed there was further support for the view that δ and C fibres are involved. Referring back to the study by Foerster and Gagel (1932), when the ventrolateral column of the spinal cord (known now as the ventral spinothalamic tract) is severed, it results not only in 'analgesia and thermoanaesthesia' on the opposite side but also absence of the sensation of tickling (Zotterman, 1939b, p. 23).

Placing these findings together, the picture from Zotterman's research is that 'fast and fat' β (and, to a lesser extent, thinly myelinated $\delta_1$and δ_2) nerve fibres that terminate in the skin are associated with fine-grained and fast (discriminative) touch, and are separate and distinct from the 'thin and slow' C nerve fibres that deal with temperature, 'burning' pain, tickling and itching routed from the skin which then enter the spinothalamic tract, that is, the spinal cord and thence to corresponding brain regions. These are all afferent nerves, reporting difference in perceptual states from the peripheral nervous system back to the brain, as opposed to efferent nerves, which coordinate and effect movements of limbs and so carry information outwards to the peripheral nervous system. For those nerves that Zotterman identified, C fibres have the lowest level (or 'spike') of signal and are by far the slowest in terms of rate of conduction (circa 2 metres per second), and are far thinner, not having the fatty insulating sheath around them that aids conductivity (i.e. in modern parlance, unmyelinated). On the other end of the spectrum, β fibres are myelinated, much wider as measured in μ (micrometers), with far higher potentials and far faster in terms of conduction (circa 60 m/s). In other words, whereas C afferents are thin and slow, β afferents are fat and fast. This is significant in terms of the types of touching that excite the different nerves. Consequently, whereas β fibres respond quickly and accurately to the usual form of touch we are labelling 'discriminative', Zotterman identifies C fibres as responding to a different form of touching altogether, as ‘a firm stroke excites fibres of very different dimensions’ (Zotterman, 1939b, p. 6).

Let us examine this instance of firm stroking, an experiment present within both 1939 papers. The measurement of action potentials across the range of nerve fibres (β, δ_1 and δ_2, C) is made when the edge of a wooden pin of 1.5 mm diameter is impressed upon the skin, and for a few seconds thereafter. The resulting graph, split in time between the action of a firm stroke with the pin, the after-effects three seconds later and then the sensation of light burning afterwards, demonstrate a sequence of the different fibres identified (see Figure 2). After an initial wave with large spike heights of β, there is an after-discharge of both $\delta_1$and δ_2 and after that C, a few seconds after withdrawal of the tactile stimulus. Given the different rates of conduction of the fibres, and following the pattern of pain, it is predictable that C fibres only emerge as an after-discharge, but then, in combination with δ_2, throughout the light burning sensation (see Zotterman, 1939b, p. 6). As Zotterman explains, such pronounced variation of different spike heights ‘indicates that a firm stroke excites fibres of very different dimensions’ (Zotterman, 1939a, p. 6; 1939b, p. 93). Contrast this frenetic activity starting with large spike heights across the fibres after firm stroking to the weaker touch involved in brushing with cotton wool, for example. In the case of light touch, the profile of action potential activity is very different, with

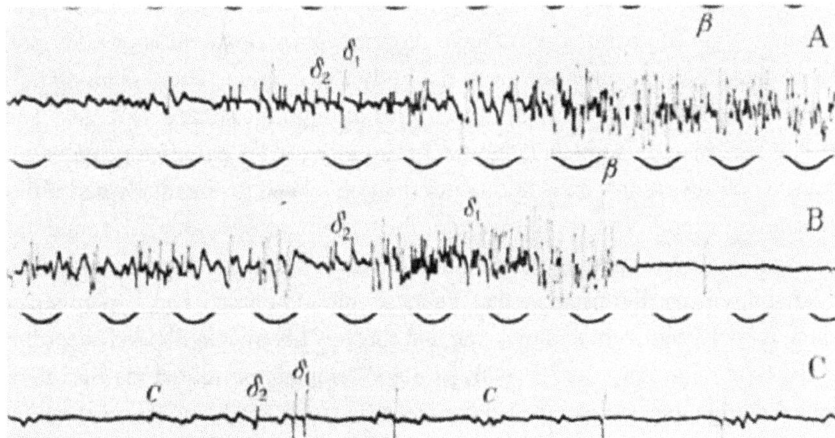

Figure 2 Graph of the action potentials after firm stroking of skin with a wooden pin, to be read from top right to bottom left as a sequence. At point A is the stroke, B is the same record three seconds later, and C is the ‘light burning’ sensation that follows. The potentials of C fibres emerge after three seconds and thereafter, in combination with δ_1 and δ_2 fibres. Reproduced from Zotterman (1939a), p. 6 with permission.

'only δ_2 potentials, often followed by a weak after-discharge of C potentials' (Zotterman, 1939a, p. 94). Clearly, Zotterman's studies are instrumental in revealing the role of the slow-conducting unmyelinated C fibres which are activated in the aftermath of firm stroking, in the burning sensation which results from this stroking, or in exposure to high temperature.

1.2 Rediscovering Earlier Nerve Pathways: C-Tactile (CT) Afferents

To understand the basic pathways of the various nerve fibres discussed so far through the mammalian body, a brief explanation at this point might be helpful to the reader as the locus shifts to the human neurophysiology of touch. From peripheral areas of mammalian vertebrate bodies, the outward surfaces of the body, afferent nerve fibres are routed through the spinal cord, up to the brainstem, and from there continue to various parts of the cerebrum, the main bulk of the brain. A major waypoint is the thalamus, a roughly four-inch-long egg-shaped concentration of grey matter located in the central area of the cerebrum, which works as a sensory and motor relay. From there, nerve signals continue to other brain areas including the somatosensory cortex on the external layer of the cerebrum. Within the spinal cord, below the brainstem, there are two pathways which deal with touch. The dorsal column-medial lemniscal pathway (DCML), often referred to simply as the dorsal column pathway, is a crucial neural pathway responsible for transmitting detailed and precise sensory information related to fine (discriminative) touch, proprioception (awareness of body position) and vibration sensation from the body to the brain. There is an entirely separate yet related pathway of nerve fibres through the spine.

The anterolateral spinothalamic tract primarily carries pain, temperature and crude touch sensations, transmitting information related to potentially harmful or threatening stimuli. Both pathways contribute to somatosensation. The anterolateral spinothalamic tract is a neural pathway involved in the transmission of the kinds of sensory information that Foerster and Zotterman had experimented upon, namely pain, temperature, itch and touch. This tract is divided according to the type of sensory nerves, with pain and temperature routed via the lateral spinothalamic tract (i.e. to one side of the spine), and touch and pressure via the anterior spinothalamic tract (front of the spine, see Figure 3). Lower down the spine, the Aδ and C fibres emerge from this anterolateral spinothalamic tract to form circuits to the skin to detect and then relay information about pain, temperature, itch and touch. This is a crude summary, as the nerve fibres involved are split between columns distributed predominantly between the anterior (front) and ventrolateral (middle) parts of the spinal column, but also marginally in the

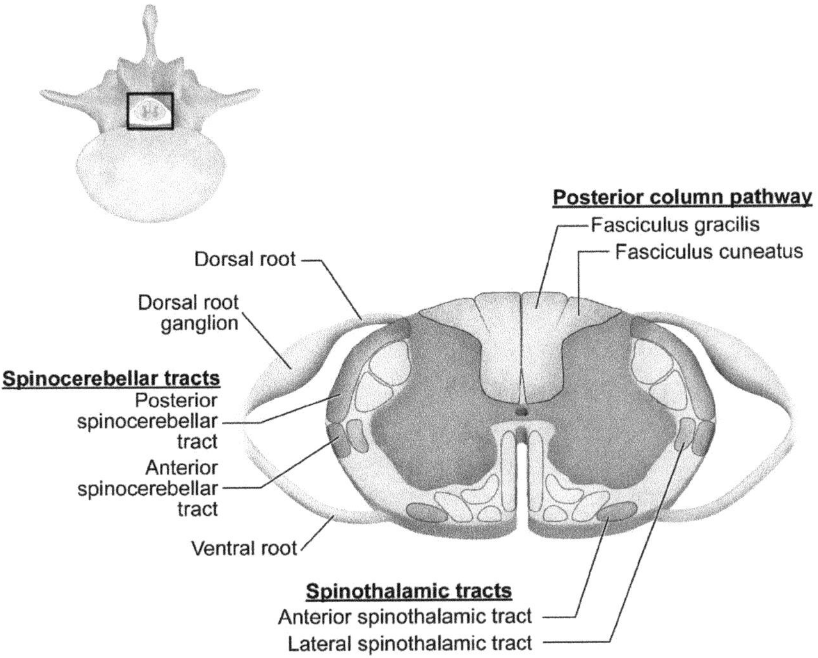

Figure 3 Sensory Pathways and Ascending Tracts in the Spinal Cord. Illustration by Bruce Blaus (2017) depicting the spinal cord's sensory pathways. **Source**: Wikimedia Commons. Copyright: CCSA-4.0.

posterior (the rearward protuberances known as the 'dorsal horn'), which has also become associated with somatosensory information. In fact, Foerster and Gagel had postulated that transmissions from nociceptors (detecting pain) and thermoreceptors (detecting temperature) also travelled through the dorsal horn. At the time they could offer no physiological evidence, so 'their proposals for the origin of the ventrolateral systems concerned with pain and temperature sensations did not receive wide acceptance', explains Perl (1971, p. 285). Subsequently, the presence of nociceptors and thermoreceptors in this area was conclusively demonstrated. Perl's paper on the distinctness of pain as a sensation (see also Paterson, 2019, 2021, p. 83ff) is notable at the time of publication in 1971 because, rather unusually, it also refers back to the research of Zotterman and his discovery of the slowly conducting unmyelinated fibres in relation to burning sensations, and specifically mentions the 'excitation of afferent units with fibers conducting in the same velocity range by the most gentle mechanical stimulation of the skin' (Perl, 1971, p. 275). This is a brief mention in passing of the connection between C-fibres and touch in service of Perl's main focus, the role of C fibres in nociception. He continues: 'Cutaneous receptors with afferent fibers of slow conduction that are responsive to innocuous manipulation have been repeatedly described', with a short series of citations of previous studies on mammals in the 1950s and 1960s, including by Zotterman continuing his work on cats, but also rats and dogs, in Stockholm with Juro Iriuchijima (Iriuchijima & Zotterman, 1960), and Ainsley Iggo in Edinburgh (Iggo, 1960), working with cats.

After Foerster in Breslau paved the way in 1932, and Zotterman was able to identity the specific role of C fibres in firm stroking of cats in Stockholm in 1939, research continued on mammals in the 1950s and 1960s. However, the detection of unmyelinated C fibres in primates did not occur until the late 1970s, where they were found to be less numerous than in the cat (Kumazawa & Perl, 1977). It would be more than a decade after this that research on nerve fibres in the human face, first by Roland Johansson in Umeå (Johansson et al., 1988) and then by Magnus Nordin in Uppsala (Nordin, 1990), picked up on the role of C fibres for human subjects again. The ability to move from experiments on nerve fibres in cats to experiments on humans was facilitated by the development of microneurogaphy. Vallbo, one of the pioneers of this technique, explains that 'the term microneurography has come to be reserved for the technique of recording impulses in human nerves using percutaneously inserted needle electrodes' (Vallbo, 2018, p. 1416). More precisely, it is a technique 'which enabled the study of axonal responses in humans via the insertion of a microelectrode through the skin into a peripheral nerve', as Schirmer et al. (2023, p. 2) put it. Although Zotterman had technically coined the term 'microneurography' in conversation with others as early as 1939 (Vallbo, 2018, p. 1416), as a technique it was not developed into its currently recognized form until 1965 by Åke Vallbo and Karl-Erik Hagbarth in Uppsala (Vallbo & Hagbarth, 1968). No longer having to physically separate out nerve fibres from living, breathing mammals to test their action potentials, Johansson et al. (1988) were therefore able to conduct a series of measurements by inserting needle electrodes into the infraorbital nerve around the human eyeball (the lower eyelid, skin and mucous membranes of the cheek and upper lip). To measure the nerves' response to pressure on the skin, he also used calibrated von Frey hairs 'to apply mechanical stimuli to the skin of the face and oral mucosa', along with 'blunt glass probes' rather than Zotterman's wooden ones (Johansson et al., 1988, p. 204).

Using microneurography in this way, Johansson found one low threshold mechanoreceptive afferent in particular had a long latency response and slow after-discharge, and speculated that it was unmyelinated: 'One slowly adapting cutaneous afferent in the present sample may have been a non-myelinated C-fiber as judged from the exceptionally long delay between the mechanical stimulation and the recorded nerve response' (Johansson et al., 1988, p. 208). They noted similarities in the characteristics with unmyelinated afferents found in studies of the hairy skin of cats and primates. Two years later, Nordin confirmed the presence of those unmyelinated afferents, and found 'receptive fields' with what he termed 'supraorbital afferent C units' around the forehead and above the eyes which responded with peak firing rates after gentle stroking (Nordin, 1990, p. 233). Like with Zotterman, Nordin found a period of after-discharges with these fibres which he timed to last around eleven seconds. While C fibres associated with nociception (pain) are high threshold, as they require a large amount of indentation or perturbance on the skin to trigger, the C fibres Nordin found were low threshold, 'of a type which has not previously been identified with certainty in man', and which gave 'preferential sensitivity to slowly moving mechanical stimuli' (Nordin, 1990, p. 238). Since Kumazawa and Perl had found C mechanoreceptors less numerous in primates than in cats, it would be reasonable for Nordin to presume that 'the C mechanoreceptors, being 'primitive' sense organs, are comparatively rare in man' (Nordin, 1990, p. 238). But how wrong he would turn out to be.

The discovery of low threshold C fibres in human skin offered a glimpse of a future research pathway, as Håkan Olausson, Johan Wessberg, Åke Vallbo and Ulf Norssell in Gothenburg, Sweden, wrote a short landmark paper about unmyelinated C fibres in the skin of the arm based on Johansson et al. and Nordin's studies on the facial nerves. The Gothenburg team's paper was the first to reveal that 'low-threshold C-fibre afferents are fairly common in the hairy skin of the forearm, suggesting that the human body is provided with a widespread system for innocuous mechanoreception subserved by unmyelinated afferents' (Vallbo et al., 1993, p. 301), 'innocuous' meaning this was about light touch as opposed to pain, which is usually described in the literature as noxious stimuli. At this stage the C fibres in question are referred to as C-mechanoreceptors, not yet as C-tactile or CT afferents. Light touch was performed through stroking the arms of human subjects using a mixture of the charmingly low-tech instruments used in studies from prior decades, including wooden probes as used in Zotterman's earlier research, and von Frey filaments. But a more high-tech microneurographic technique was used in this study by Vallbo. Initial findings echoed those of Zotterman and his cats, with two sets of responses detected around the stroking, one involving instantaneous response with 'low-latency units' (myelinated fibres), and another a delayed response with 'long-latency units' identified as unmyelinated afferents. Both systems were invoked in the sensitivity to 'moving touch stimuli', but the focus for the paper was solidly on the latter, leading to the conclusion that 'it seems clear that our sample of long-latency units are unmyelinated afferents with a high sensitivity to light touch', and that such units were relatively abundant, constituting around 40 per cent of the units in that area of the forearm (Vallbo et al., 1993, p. 303). For the receptive fields in the skin that respond to low threshold touch, 'there can be no doubt that they constitute a different type of sensory element than the mechanosensitive nociceptors previously described in the hairy skin of human limbs' (Vallbo et al., 1993, p. 303). What was this 'widespread system', a separate form of light touch in humans, and why was it ignored for so long? Their only explanation at this early stage in the discovery is brief and unsubstantiated: 'it has been suggested that an older and slowly conducting system for innocuous mechanoreception has faded away during evolutionary processes antedating man' (Vallbo et al., 1993, p. 301).

1.2.1 C-Tactile (CT) Afferents: Their Function and Purpose

Olausson and the team were already aware in 1988 of unmyelinated (unsheathed) C nerve fibres in humans, but their purpose was entirely unknown until the turn of the millennium (Vallbo et al., 1999; Wessberg et al., 2003), which boosted the evidence for an entire secondary, low-threshold tactile system attuned to affective response. This circuit of nerves, separate from the high-speed myelinated Aβ fibres which functioned for discriminatory touch, became C-tactile (or CT) afferents. As one of the original papers on this topic admitted, at first the functional role of CT afferents was not known, and so the hypothesis of an affective touch system began. Translating Zotterman's identification of fibres (β, δ_1 and δ_2, C) into the Erlanger-Gasser classification of myelinated Group A nerves (e.g. Aβ and Aδ) and unmyelinated Group C nerves (especially C-tactile, or 'CT'), the early data suggested that Aβ (i.e. discriminative, high speed) and CT are separate systems with connections to different cortical areas. Now that the surprising evidence for this C-fibre touch system in human skin had been verified and shown to be so extensive, questions as to its function could be asked. In their 1993 paper, Vallbo et al. can only venture that its function is separate from the cognitive processing of skin contact of the low-latency fibres. Instead, they speculate:

> Maybe the system has its main role in its relationship to subcortical structures in the brain, e.g. to limbic and hypothalamic functions. There are indications from animal experiments that tactile afferents may have a variety of effects within this realm of functions, notably control over hormonal systems which might be of particular significance for the development of the infant. (Vallbo et al., 1993, p. 304)

It is this direction that a series of later studies with various combinations of members of the Gothenburg lab and their co-authors follow. For example, another landmark paper written in 1999 by Gothenburg colleagues Vallbo, Olausson and Wessberg (Vallbo et al., 1999), and a 2002 paper in *Nature Neuroscience* (Olausson et al., 2002) which ventured further into the realm of social touch and was widely reported in the media. This work has led to the formulation of what has been termed the 'affective touch hypothesis' (Ellingsen et al., 2015; McGlone et al., 2014; Olausson et al., 2010; Vallbo et al., 1999) or, alternatively, the 'social touch hypothesis' of India Morrison (Morrison, 2016b, 2023). These hypotheses are discussed more fully in the following section. Needless to say, however, the Swedish research boosted the evidence for an entire secondary, low-threshold tactile system attuned to affective response. This is the C-low threshold mechanoreceptors (CLTMs), as distinguished from nociceptive (pain related) C-high threshold mechanoreceptors (CHTMs).

As we know from Zotterman, the group C nerves respond to a range of stimuli including burning, itching, and pain. The C-tactile (or CT) afferent is predominantly mechanosensitive, responding optimally to gentle, moving touch at skin temperature, around 32 degrees centigrade (Ackerley et al., 2014; Morrison, 2016b). 'The properties of CT afferents include maximal firing to slow-velocity stroking at low forces, small receptive fields with sensitive hot spots, and a slow conduction velocity relating to the unmyelinated axon', says Ackerley et al. (2014, p. 2879). The firing frequency of these CT fibres correlates with subjective ratings of pleasantness, as Morrison explains, so: 'Human CT afferents also display a 'tuning curve' for caressing speeds that people find most pleasant' (2016b, p. 360). For recent animal studies as well as for humans, the activation of CT fibres is associated with 'hedonic effects' but also 'anxiolytic effects', that is, the reduction of anxiety (Ackerley et al., 2014, p. 2879). These findings further underline the significance of the role of CT afferents in social touch (Olausson et al., 2010).

1.2.2 The 'Affective Touch' and 'Social Touch' Hypotheses

One of the first high-profile publications by the team in Gothenburg, the paper in *Nature Neuroscience* (Olausson et al., 2002), was picked up by news agencies, and the association between more emotional forms of touching and the newly rediscovered unmyelinated 'slow' fibres resonated with the public. What popular news outlets and magazines could ignore stories that purported to scientifically explain these intimate, nurturing, and of course erotic forms of touching at last? For example, the BBC News website profiled Olausson and his team's research with the title 'Lover's touch is special' (BBC, 2002). At first, as one of the original papers on this topic admitted, the functional role of these CT afferents was not known (Olausson et al., 2002, p. 900), hence the hypothesis of affective touch began. The early data suggested 'that A and CT are separate systems with different connections to cortical areas', and, unlike the A system, 'the CT system does not provide discriminative aspects of touch' (Olausson et al., 2002, p. 902). Rather, the CT system provides only vague awareness of tactile stimuli in terms of cutaneous location and duration of stroking.

The initial data was compiled with the help of a single significant case study referred to as 'G.L.', who subsequently features often in the literature on affective touch. In 2002 G.L. was a fifty-four-year-old female test subject who had the rare pathological condition that, because of disease from the age of thirty-one, suffered loss of all her large-diameter myelinated nerve fibres, including those for touch. It is because of this rare neuronopathy (a disorder of the peripheral nervous system) that fMRI scans could target unique cortical activity for CT fibres alone, whereas for most 'normal' test subjects there would additionally be cortical activity through discriminative touching. Incidentally, in a charming historical throwback, G.L.'s tactile capacities were tested in much the same way as in Weber or Fechner's psychophysics laboratory, with moving brushes and self-reporting by the test subject. The core of the affective touch hypothesis at this early stage was: 'The CT system may thus be of importance for emotional, hormonal (for example, oxytocin) and behavioral responses to tactile stimulation' (Olausson et al., 2002, p. 902), which has been an enduring factor through later literature also, and will open the gateway to considering neurochemical and developmental aspects of social touch.

A follow-up study by a team involving Olausson, this time with the neurologist Jonathan Cole, had the benefit of introducing another case study alongside G.L. (Olausson et al., 2008). I.W. had a rare sensory neuronopathy involving touch, and effectively had to relearn how to walk and move his limbs through a series of orchestrated actions and with great concentration. I.W. had featured in studies by Jonathan Cole, and was central to his book *Pride and a Daily Marathon* (Cole, 1995), as I.W. also lacked Aβ afferents, greatly affecting his interoception, the term Sherrington had coined. A later paper by McGlone, Wessberg and Olausson sees how the two distinct nervous pathways, the discriminative and the affective, must be combined for pleasant touch sensation: 'The combination of CT and Aβ afferents is required for the complete feeling of pleasant touch in the hairy skin, and the intensity and even the quality of the emotional response evoked by a particular stimulus is highly dependent on contextual factors' (McGlone et al., 2014, p. 749).

What has become known in some circles as the 'affective touch hypothesis' (Ellingsen et al., 2015; McGlone et al., 2014; Vallbo et al., 1999; Vallbo et al., 2009), and for others the 'social touch hypothesis' (Morrison et al., 2010; Olausson et al., 2010), has become more accepted in the neuroscience literature in the past two decades. The social touch hypothesis is explained as the result of the anatomical peculiarity and the slow response characteristics of the C low-threshold mechanoreceptors (CLTMs), compared to the faster, large-diameter Aβ fibres, as Francis McGlone and Susannah Walker explain:

> their force, temperature and velocity tuning appear to make them ideally suited to form the first stage of encoding socially relevant and rewarding tactile information resulting from affiliative behaviors, suggesting that CLTMs may have an evolutionarily conserved function in the formation and maintenance of social bonds (McGlone & Walker, 2020, p. 73)

Elsewhere, for example in an *Encyclopedia of Neuroscience* entry 'Pleasant Touch' by Vallbo, Olausson and Wessberg, three of the original pioneering researchers in Gothenburg on C-tactile afferents in humans, explain it in more hedonic terms: 'the essential role of the CT system is to convey pleasant aspects of light touch, particularly of skin-to-skin contact with affiliative human beings' (Vallbo et al., 2009, p. 744). The neutral use of the terms 'affiliative' and 'conspecifics', in this publication and others, refers for example to the touch between human parents and infant offspring, and between sexually mature lovers, but also between mammals that exhibit grooming behaviours. Yet, even within the publication by Vallbo, Olausson and Wessberg which had celebrated the scientific basis of 'pleasant touch', they also explicitly declared: 'this does not imply that CT-afferents are the only afferents that may contribute or give rise to limbic touch effects' (Vallbo et al., 2009, p. 744). This observation was followed up in a separate section on fMRI imaging of brain responses to touch stimuli, where the absence of CT-afferents but the presence of Aβ afferents in smooth, hairless parts of the body like the palm of the hand nonetheless registers in the insular cortex, associated with the emotional system. This leads the authors to conclude something which could be easily missed in media reporting, and which seems to contradict the claim of distinct affective and discriminative tactile systems: 'The combination of CT- and Aβ-afferents is obviously required for the complete feeling of pleasant touch in the hairy skin' (Vallbo et al., 2009, p. 746). Referring to this admission that it is not only CT afferents but also Aβ afferents that contribute to limbic touch effects, Schirmer et al. observe: 'Notably, this [. . .] point has often gone unnoticed in subsequent work' (2023, p. 2).

The rather neat distinction formulated in the early years of the novel research on CT-afferents helped to stimulate much-needed interest within the scientific community but also, as we saw, more broadly in the news media, as we saw with the uptake of the *Nature Neuroscience* paper. However, doubts have existed for some time about the assumed split between the functions of touch and the different afferents involved. Is this distinction between the role of discriminative touch and affective touch, between the systems of Aβ and CT afferents, quite so neatly separated in actuality? Some researchers such as Francis McGlone (McGlone et al., 2014) have claimed the two distinct nervous pathways work together in order that pleasant touch sensation is felt. A recent paper in *Neuroscience and Behavioral Reviews* on CT afferents by established scholars Annette Schirmer, Ilona Croy, and Rochelle Ackerley (Schirmer et al., 2023) also explicitly addresses this assumed separation, and discusses studies over the years that categorically demonstrate how and why this picture is not so straightforward. Furthermore, the authors gathered an expert group of fellow neuroscientists to discuss the use of academic language in published papers and abstracts where there was a significant overlap between the concepts of positive affects and 'CT' or 'C-tactile' afferents, yet within the online meeting of neuroscientists, 'the majority of our expert group defined affective touch as something going beyond the activation of CTs' (Schirmer et al., 2023, p. 6). Why has there been this 'striking gap', as they put it, between the published academic literature and expert views on the neuroscience? One answer is that, like in any rapidly developing but complex field, communicating to a broad audience tends to simplify the picture, and of course scientists are reliant on funding by taxpayers. The early studies which brought forth the 'affective touch' hypothesis captured the public imagination for a reason.

1.3 Social Touch 'in the Wild'

Questions about the 'why?' of affective touch behaviours could only be asked tentatively during the early phases of the identification and measurement, the 'what' and 'how' respectively, of CT afferents in humans and primates especially. Key to this question is the motivation to communicate nonverbally. How do the different nerve fibres including CT afferents function in more messy entanglements of sensory information and contextually dependent emotional content 'in the wild', that is, outside of strictly controlled laboratory conditions, and with fellow humans as opposed to prods, probes and artificial touching tools? In their review of scientific literature on the communication of affective touch, Merle Fairhurst, Francis McGlone and Ilona Croy put this issue straightforwardly: 'studies have focused on the behavioural, physiological and neural responses to receiving affective touch with relatively little known about the benefits or motivation that drives us to reach out and touch someone else, or to seek touch from someone else' (Fairhurst et al., 2022, p. 54). They identify a related tendency in laboratory studies of affective touch to concentrate on the receiving of touch, as opposed to investigating subjects who provide affective touch, that is, reach out and make contact with skin areas with concentrations of CT afferents, such as the arms and back, through stroking or hugging. We return to their model of CT-mediated communication later in this section, but first I offer selected highlights of classic studies of communication and grooming behaviours in social settings, before discussing how recent research in this area directly incorporates the neurophysiological discoveries of C-tactile pathways and areas of CT innervation.

Outside of the neuroscience, of course, something akin to the 'affective touch hypothesis' or the 'social touch hypothesis' has been present and actively researched for decades outside of scientific laboratories, including most prominently in social psychology and studies of nonverbal communication. The significance of touch for interpersonal communication, especially, and the role of grooming behaviours involving touch contact and slow stroking to promote social bonds between individuals and promote cooperation has long been observed and explored in mammals, primates and humans to varying extents. For the purposes of this short Element, only a brief overview of selected classic studies on the power of interpersonal touch in the nonverbal communication and social psychology literatures is provided, but especially notable are those that dwell specifically on the role of slow touch in fostering prosocial bonding behaviours. A number of breakout studies in psychology beginning in the late 1950s through to the 1970s started to support such observations, including Harry Harlow and his landmark research with rhesus macaques on maternal physical contact (Harlow, 1958), and Ashley Montagu and his extensive monograph reviewing touch research until the late 1960s (Montagu, 1971), extended for its third edition (Montagu, 1986). In terms of researching the role of touch in communication, Jeffrey Fisher and colleagues conducted an early investigation of affective touch between people, and Richard Heslin and Tari Alper on the role of touch in social bonding (Fisher et al., 1976; Heslin & Alper, 1982). A snapshot of this increasingly productive research on touch was conducted by Stephen Thayer (1986) in the then relatively new *Journal of Nonverbal Behavior*, whose first issue came out in 1976. Also around that time, Stanley Jones and A. Elaine Yarbrough (1985) produced a typology of twelve distinct meanings of touch encounters they had observed in everyday life encounters, while Judee Burgoon also looked at what is communicated within touch interactions and noted correlations with posture and proximity factors. Building on her previous collaborative research, Burgoon also demonstrated that different forms of touch have different 'relational meanings'; that is, they help in 'defining and clarifying the status of interpersonal relationships' (1991, p. 234). These meanings are shared by the majority of a culture in a so-called 'social meaning model', where for example a handshake indicates a formal relationship whereas a hug indicates an informal one. It is the types of touch which escape explicit social meaning, yet where there are observable behavioural effects, that is increasingly of interest to HRI researchers. For example, tracking the nonconscious promotion of pro-social behaviours or compliance, or increases in the human perception of trust. As Laura Hoffman and Nicole Krämer summarize, 'a variety of studies have demonstrated that people are more willing to comply with a request if the person asking a favour uses touch (e.g., participate in a course; help an experimenter after the original experiment; sign a petition; lend a dime; look after a dog)' (2021, p. 3). According to Fisher, Rytting and Heslin (Fisher et al., 1976), for touch to have positive effects, it has to convey a message of care and concern, and match the level of intimacy preferred by the recipient. 'This adds a cognitive-interpretational dimension to the experience of touch', explain Hoffman and Krämer. 'If a positive interpretation and preferred level of intimacy are not given, interpersonal touch is rather undesirable and can result in rejection' (Hoffmann & Krämer, 2021, p. 4)

In light of this, it is important to acknowledge that not all touching behaviours are positive, and powerful associations and reactions to the touch of other people can arise without positive effects. Barely noticed, brief or light touching in interactions with strangers can lead to ambiguities. Conscious and unconscious tactile contact was central to April Crusco and Christopher Wetzel's classic study of restaurant tipping behaviour, for example, where customers were lightly touched either on the hand or on the shoulder by waiters when receiving change after paying (Crusco & Wetzel, 1984). An earlier example of this ambiguity in nonverbal communication occurs in a study by Fisher, Rytting and Heslin (1976), who observed what happens when librarians briefly touched visitors' hands when returning their library cards. The effects of briefly adding light touch to the interaction was subsequently reported as both positive and negative. Only 57 per cent of the respondents were consciously aware of being touched in the interaction, but the general trend effect for both male and female visitors was a more positive evaluation of the interaction: 'The multivariate analysis of the dependent measures revealed a main effect for touch, which indicated that subjects in touch conditions evidenced more positive responses than subjects in no touch conditions'. However, their finding of ambiguity in the reception of touch by users is exacerbated by the uneven levels of familiarity with nonverbal conventions in haptics and proxemics across different cultures and even spatial contexts, for example at work, in public spaces or at home. This situation is further complicated by the variability of competencies in identifying and responding to nonverbal communication channels within human populations, especially those with autism spectrum conditions (ASC). This variability in the interpretation of touch behaviours will become significant again in the following sections' discussion of technology and the mediation of touch.

A recent model of the role of touch in interpersonal communication explicitly takes account of CT afferents as well as Aβ afferents is offered by Fairhurst, McGlone and Croy. It involves findings from two of the authors, McGone and Croy, who are neuroscientists we have previously encountered who have worked on CT afferents. Together with a philosopher of science (not a communication scholar), they posit a CT-mediated touch system where messages are sent through a 'channel' or sensory route to be received, 'the channel for the invaluable transmission of affective content mediated by the CT afferent system' (Fairhurst et al., 2022, p. 54). The kind of tactile content that stimulates this channel includes single instances of touch such as a stroke on the shoulder, the kinds of nonverbal behaviour discussed in historical studies, but also reciprocal and ritualized exchanges such as rubbing noses or a hug. Based on prior microneurographic mapping data which shows the density of CT afferents, they identify zones or areas on the body which are more effective for this type of affective touch communication than others. Now, although in the previous section the distinction between the functions of CT afferents as 'affective' and Aβ afferents as 'discriminative' became less absolute, with some acknowledgement of functional integration between them, there remains a key neurophysiological difference in terms of speed of innervation and transmission between unmyelinated CT-mediated touch and myelinated Aβ-mediated touch which actually works together as a whole. It remains the case that 'the information that is communicated by the slow CT system, rather than descriptive or informational, is evaluative and motivational', they argue (Fairhurst et al., 2022, p. 56). But with a more integrative model of affective touch, the CT afferents might not have an exclusive or unitary role in affective tactile coding, they continue, but instead shape the neural outputs of the ascending dorsal horn (conducting somatosensory information, see beginning Section 1.2). If so, as Marshall and McGlone (2020) claim elsewhere, the full expression of affective touch is reliant on input not just from CT afferents but also through the faster discriminative system (Aβ) as well. In addition, the optimal speed of stroking was described previously (beginning Section 1.2) through CT innervation as an inverted-U shaped curve, with lower response if stroking was too fast or too slow. Interestingly, as Haggarty et al. (2020) found, individual differences like autistic quotient have been shown to modify this curve response.

Combining or reassembling such behavioural observations of slow or social touching with physiological measurements and neurochemical aspects has provided concrete evidence for the way that affective touching benefits health and well-being. As Morrison explains: 'Prosocial touch can be defined as intentional social touch that benefits the "touchee" via physiological regulation of bodily responses' (Morrison, 2016b, p. 354). Slow or nurturing forms of touch in humans have been linked to reduced stress, increased trust between interactants and enhanced well-being, and plays a significant role in fostering prosocial behaviour. Harlow's previously mentioned research, offering macaque offspring either wire or terry cloth covered versions of their mothers, memorably demonstrated the importance of tactile contact, what he termed 'contact comfort', for primate development. The data supported his claim that 'contact comfort is a variable of overwhelming importance in the development of affectional responses' (Harlow, 1958, p. 676), even overriding the instinctive need for feeding. Thereafter, a number of psychologists studied the role of touch in human infant development, including Mary Ainsworth (1979). The effects of long-term touch deprivation in humans has been documented, leading to devastating consequences, as the work of Tiffany Field in the 1990s and 2000s explored (e.g. Field, 2001, 2014). A notorious example that Field mentions is the case of the Romanian orphanages under President Nicolai Ceaușescu. Ceaușescu's government in the 1980s not only banned abortions in order to increase the nation's population but also institutionalized a large number of infants with perceived disabilities and bodily deformities. A population of abandoned newborn infants were kept in large state-run orphanages, rooms filled with rows of isolated cribs, malnourished and with minimal human interaction. They stayed underweight and underdeveloped. Scientific evidence shows the extent of developmental problems that ensue from touch deprivation, including disruption of growth (due to disturbances in growth hormones), suppressed immune response, sleep disturbance, aversion to touch and even increased physical violence (Field, 2014, p. 74ff). Field set up a Touch Research Institute at the University of Miami School of Medicine in 1992 to address some of these problems. A notable study by Field and others published in 1986 found that premature infants had healthier outcomes by putting on weight more rapidly, and doing better in developmental tasks, if they were gently massaged by nurses for forty-five minutes a day, broken up into fifteen-minute periods over ten days (Field et al., 1986). With some preterm infants being given either lighter touch or no touch at all, as Field explains elsewhere, 'The babies who gained weight had been given deeper pressure massage, thus stimulating both tactile and pressure receptors (specialized nerve endings that respond to pressure)' (2014, p. 147). Bearing in mind Field's use of simplified scientific terminology for a non-specialist readership, it can be assumed that CT afferents are stimulated in those massage interactions as opposed to merely mechanoreceptors that respond to pressure. The fact that this paediatric research on the benefits of touch, as well as the social scientific studies on the role of touch in nonverbal communication, emerged decades ago makes it even more surprising that the neurophysiological explanations behind such findings are so comparatively recent.

The effects of touch, and touch deprivation, on responses to stress by an organism are part of what underlines Harlow's research on primates and Field's research on human pre-term and full-term infants, among others. What drives this need for tactile contact (or Harlow's 'contact comfort')? As Schirmer et al. venture, citing studies from 2008 onwards, 'there is some indication that gentle touch may be relevant for promoting pro-social processes and the developing social brain with causal evidence from non-human animals [. . .] and correlational evidence from humans' (2023, p. 2). The neurochemical effects of affective touch, particularly the release of the hormones cortisol and oxytocin, have been known for decades. For example, Field explains the results of a study from 1993: 'Blood samples were obtained for stress-hormone (cortisol) levels forty-five minutes before the start of the massage and approximately one hour after the end of the massage. The cortisol levels consistently decreased after the massage' (Field, 2014, p. 150). This observation was later verified in a study by Field and her team, who also tracked increased levels of dopamine and serotonin levels in infants (Field et al., 2005). The neurodevelopmental effects of social touch and its deprivation are still being actively mapped, most recently by neuroimaging studies, but it is clear that such links between social touch and neurochemical phenomena are crucial throughout various mammalian developmental phases. Recently, Schirmer et al. reviewed some studies which showed that touch at 'CT optimal stroking velocities (i.e. gentle moving touch delivered around 1–10 cm/s)' reduces pain response in full-term infants and reduces heart rate in pre-term and full-term infants, and is therefore 'suited to change an infant's interoceptive state and to promote homeostasis' (2023, p. 2). McGlone and Walker (2020) echo Field's findings about the effects of social touch deprivation, and find and cite a range of studies on the role of 'CLTM-optimal touch' (i.e. slow touch involving CT afferents) and its deprivation on infant development. Studies on rodents for example show modifications of allostatic load and therefore stress response, as tactile licking and grooming behaviours invite the release of oxytocin, an endogenous antidepressant. On the other hand, long-term touch deprivation de-regulates the hypothalamic-pituitary-axis (HPA), and maternal separation is known to heighten HPA, and even 'hinder the development of cortical regions involved in the HPA responses', explain McGlone and Walker (2020, p. 74). In other words, long-term social touch deprivation at key neurodevelopmental stages limits the individual organism's responses to stress by actually modifying the formation of the brain regions responsible for stress response in the first place. In addition, the kinds of nurturing touch that mothers provide to offspring, what McGlone and Walker term 'CLTM-optimal dynamic touch', have beneficial effects on their offspring through increasing the infant's parasympathetic arousal, meaning that mammals become calmer and lower their heartrate, a complementary and counteracting response to the sympathetic nervous system's arousal due to stress (or, in simpler terms, 'rest-digest' as opposed to 'fight-flight' responses).

India Morrison, a pioneer scientist who has investigated CT afferents and published with the Gothenburg team, argues that one of the ways that affective-motivational functions of touch are separated from the discriminative function is that the hedonic or pleasurable aspects of slow touch are key to the domain of social interactions. What makes this touch feel pleasant to the organism? Furthering Field's earlier exploratory research involving measuring cortisol levels, a more complex neurochemistry involving touch is being mapped, and the release of oxytocin during childbirth, breastfeeding and sexual activity has been regarded as promoting feelings of bonding with others. 'Tactile stimulation is a major trigger for oxytocin release, especially for uterine contraction in labor, and milk ejection in lactation and breastfeeding', explains Morrison, but also 'stimulation of sensory neurons outside a parturition context can also stimulate oxytocin release' (2016b, p. 353), such as social touch interactions with family, friends and intimate partners. A paper on the neurobiology of affective touch written by a team including Olausson and Wessberg likewise identify the role of oxytocin in stress regulation and social bonding, and previous research had confirmed its anxiety-reducing or 'anxiolyitic effects': 'it has been suggested that the soothing and anxiolytic effects of stroking touch in mammals is mediated by oxytocin' (Ellingsen et al., 2015, p. 8).

From these correlations and others, Morrison builds up a larger picture of social touch as a 'stress buffer' for an individual organism. A stress buffer is 'any mechanism or process that mitigates, attenuates, offsets, or prevents energy efficiency losses among regulatory systems, while remaining adequately responsive to external challenges' (Morrison, 2016b, p. 349). Morrison claims there are three ways that pleasant touch is used in this way for social regulation in mammals. First, as social thermoregulation, where huddling behaviours mitigate heat loss, especially in young mammals with little ability to control their own temperature. Second, the regulation of physical proximity to others through opioid and oxytocin signalling, where an animal can become stressed through separation from a mother when young, or a group when older. Third, prosocial touch, including 'allogrooming' (grooming the fur or skin of a group member) and 'consolation behaviour' (touching intended to provide comfort) (Morrison, 2016b, p. 345). What stands out about Morrison's investigation of touch and grooming in mammals here is that it goes beyond individual bodily effects, and instead builds from other scientists' observed correlations between slow touch and neurochemical release in order to collectively help regulate social distance between individuals and groups. Instead of Walter Cannon's (1939) idea of homeostatic regulation at the level of the individual organism, in other words, it involves an allostatic perspective (Sterling & Eyer, 1990) which involves other group members. Allostatic regulation keeps the body's systems within a range in which energy is neither wasted nor over-conserved in its overall responses to changing conditions. As the complex neurochemistry continues to be charted, where contact and grooming leads to the release of oxytocin, opioids, and neurotransmitters like serotonin, the role of CT afferents becomes more central for prosocial and allogrooming behaviours, which enhance nurturing and attachment behaviours in mammals. Morrison therefore postulates: 'social thermoregulation, social attachment via opioid and oxytocin signaling, and prosocial touch – may have their evolutionary origins in systems adapted for specific forms of parental nurturance and offspring attachment behavior' (2016b, p. 358).

2 Social Touch and Its Mediations: Socio-technological Applications

If the previous section had assessed some of the developmental and neurochemical effects of social touch and its deprivation, Section 2 is about the means to achieve social touch through various technologies and therefore *mediate* it. Around the world, since 2016 the heavily publicized #MeToo movement brought an awareness of the prevalence of uninvited sexualized touching and assault by men. Social touch was undergoing a heightened vigilance in the workplace even before COVID-19 lockdowns, then, and prohibitions on adults touching children at school have been in place for years across the Global North, with Tiffany Field identifying the emergence of touch as a taboo in American schools in 1995 (Field, 2014, p. 2). During the successive global pandemic lockdowns in 2020–21, existing wariness about social touch almost overnight turned into privation for many around the world. The prohibition on groups of people assembling and conducting so many forms of social interaction with each other, including eating, dating, shopping, visiting care home residents or even walking outside together, revealed the uncanny effect of the absence of social touch on a large scale. What Field memorably calls a 'touch hunger' (2001, 2014) ensued. During innumerable video and phone calls with geographically separated loved ones, with audio-visual stimuli on demand, the absence of the touch modality was keenly felt. Yet there have already been a significant number of devices envisioned by engineers, designers, and artists over the past two decades built to communicate the presence of another to oneself, to build in a haptic channel for communication.

What about the other forms of touch, then, the affective-motivational, slow or social touch, using unmyelinated CT afferents? Based on what has been argued in Section 1 so far, how have technologies facilitated social interaction and emotional communication through touch, allowed handshakes, gentle stroking, hugging or intimate caressing? Although there have been few if any commercially successful or mainstream equivalents to force feedback controllers that address the discriminative neural pathways, over the past few decades there have been a surprising number of small projects, laboratory-based devices, design projects, and tech start-ups that have arisen to address this need to communicate a meaningful and affective presence to others using touch. The next two sections offer brief examples and case studies of some of these efforts. Section 2.1 examines haptic interfaces and their role in communicating social touch at a distance, or what has come to be known as 'mediated social touch'. Section 2.2 looks at social touch in human–robot interaction, from small animal-like robots that users can stroke or hug, right up to an intimidatingly large purpose-built HuggieBot.

2.1 Social Touch at a Distance: A Virtual Handshake

Why not start with one of the most common forms of nonverbal communication involving touch, a handshake? In October 2002 newspapers reported the first 'virtual handshake', where researchers at Boston's MIT TouchLabs and London's UCL held virtual hands and manipulated virtual objects together over the internet, each using SensAble's $20,000 PHANToM (Personal HAptic iNTerface Mechanism) high fidelity desktop device (Arthur, 2002; Kim et al., 2004; Paterson, 2006, 2007). Haptic interfaces like these provide the sensation of touch by exerting accurately controlled forces on the fingers. By this means it is possible to simulate not only the shape of a virtual object but also its texture and elasticity. The experience for users at their desks so far apart, passing virtual objects that feel weighty and tangible between each other and with no appreciable latency, encourages talk of 'presence'. The term 'telepresence', coined in the history of robotics to mean the sense of presence at a distance (Sheridan, 1989), is certainly what the virtual handshake achieved. Charles Arthur, then science editor for *The Independent* newspaper, was present for the occasion and wastes no time in fantasizing about more exotic telepresence applications:

> the software used could one day mean that we will feel the sensation of objects picked up on the surface of the Moon or beneath the sea, surgeons could do operations remotely, a whole new genre of computer games could be created – internet arm-wrestling, anyone? – and perhaps a remarkable new spice could be added to internet sex. (Arthur, 2002, p. 7)

Jung Kim, one of the Ph.D. students in the MIT team, later wrote about this as 'copresence' (Kim et al., 2004), the ability to interact with another and feel their presence simultaneously. A phrase that has subsequently caught on a bit more that also refers to this type of phenomenon is 'mediated social touch' (Haans & Ijsselsteijn, 2006, 2009; Huisman, 2012). Haans and Ijsselstein describe mediated social touch as 'a sense of presence of a distant other' achieved through haptic technology, and more precisely as 'the ability of one actor to touch another actor over a distance by means of tactile or kinesthetic feedback technology' (2006, p. 153). This phrase continues to have academic currency, with journal articles, international symposia, and workshops on this theme, although Huisman in a later survey of haptic technologies used for social touch characterizes these devices as 'social touch technologies', or STT (Huisman, 2017).

Phrasing this event as a 'virtual handshake' makes good newspaper copy, of course. It was undoubtedly an achievement in telepresence with joint tasks undertaken simultaneously, but this mischaracterization of a social form of touch interaction, the handshake, is rather revealing. It opens up a preexisting rift between the technical possibilities that high-fidelity haptic interfaces can provide, and the actual social content or meaning of that interaction. This section will offer an overview of a number of different haptic technologies with a range of tactile fidelities, from basic 'buzz' and 'burr' to fully graspable and manipulatable objects in 3D space. Throughout, however, what remains paramount is the 'social' aspect of 'mediated social touch', the meanings behind the haptic interaction, and so the use of technology for nonverbal communication will feature heavily. At the other end of the haptic scale from the PHANToM, for example, is the personal consumer haptics of CuteCircuit's HugShirt. First released in 2014 with twelve 'haptic micro-actuators' (https://cutecircuit.com/hugshirt/ 2024) sewn into the fabric, it is designed to communicate a hug for geographically separated people over the internet via a smartphone app. A number of such smaller, less ambitious projects like this will be described later, but there are real limitations on the interface engineering side in terms of what can directly make contact with areas of CT innervation, with the hedonic or 'pleasant' aspects of touch discussed in Section 1.2 only unevenly captured in the ecosystem of interfaces encountered in this section. The kinds of actions such as regular, smooth stroking at particular velocities and temperature ranges that produced favourable neurochemical effects via the affective touch pathways have no equivalent to the PHANToM, which delivers stimuli to the 'discriminative' touch system via force reflectance to mimic the physical shapes and textures of a virtual object recognizably. Instead, emotional communication through haptics is predominantly achieved through lower-resolution or low-fidelity haptics, but with the emotive intent coded and decoded as patterns of vibrotactile actuation, like ComTouch (Chang, 2002) or the Hugshirt (https://cutecircuit.com/hugshirt, 2024). One key aspect of mediated social touch that Huisman identifies is attribution, so that whatever the level of fidelity of touch, whether it feels realistic or not, that touch is transmitted or sent purposefully, and that its intent is able to be discerned by the receiver:

> Mediated social touch requires detection of a touch on the end of the sender and rendering of the touch at the end of the receiver. The sender needs to be aware of the fact that his/her input causes a physical sensation at the receiver's end while the receiver needs to believe that the felt sensation is caused by the sender. (Huisman, 2017, p. 395)

Despite the technical limitations, there is evidence that mediated touch can increase pro-social, altruistic behaviour and willingness to comply with a request (Haans & Ijsselsteijn, 2009), and, as Roope Raisamo et al. summarize, can provide a sense of intimacy between geographically separated partners watching the same content, 'increase trust and affection', and 'can lower the heart rate of participants after they watch a sad video clip' (Raisamo et al., 2022, pp. 3–4). In fact, a whole area known as 'affective haptics' is 'the emerging area of research which focuses on the design of devices and systems that can elicit, enhance, or influence [the] emotional state of a human by means of sense of touch' (Tsetserukou et al., 2009, p. 1).

The story of haptic technologies, and the engineering behind other hands and presences at a distance, starts with Raymond Goertz's 1949 design for what he called a 'master-slave manipulator'. For the processing of radioactive material at the Argonne National Laboratory there was the need for remotely operated mechanical hands. In 1953 a version was built with what is known in engineering circles as 'force reflection' or haptic feedback for the human operator (the 'master' unit) through a system of wires and pulleys to better 'feel' and control an object in the 'slave' unit (Parisi, 2018, pp. 221–222). The manipulator entered production as the CRL Model 8 in 1954 and became more widely known as the Argonne Remote Manipulator (ARM). Thus began an era in which the fantasy of being able to feel and manipulate an object at a distance was now achievable through engineering expertise. Since the Greek root *τῆλε* (*tele*) means distance or afar, the engineering of Goertz's ARM is a major reason why we now have telepresence, telecare, telesurgery, even teledildonics. The tactile feedback that an operator expects in order to accomplish their task effectively involves what haptics engineers call 'force reflectance', 'force feedback', 'haptic feedback' or sometimes simply 'haptics'. The ARM achieved this through analogue technologies of wires, levers and pulleys, but modern devices use actuators and electric motors to either provide basic vibration on the skin surface or else employ exoskeletal structures or free-moving arms with motors that push back against the skin, fingers, or limbs of the user to give a sense of an object's boundaries and materials within a portion of three-dimensional space (e.g. the PHANToM and CyberGrasp glove, see Figures 4 and 5, respectively, and HaptX Gloves G1). These more advanced haptic interfaces offer a proprioceptive component for the user rather than simple cutaneous sensation, and as such can provide convincing-enough sensations for the purposes of training, such as in driving vehicles, nursing, or dentistry. Although the CyberGrasp is rather dated, released in 1998 and discontinued in 2019, how the product was envisaged in their brochure is illustrative of the concepts discussed so far:

> The CyberGrasp device is an innovative force-feedback system for your fingers and hand. A CyberGrasp system provides ungrounded (hand-referenced) force feedback to each finger and the palm, allowing you to feel computer-generated or telemanipulated objects that you 'reach into your computer' and grasp. (Brochure 2009, available at est-kl.com)

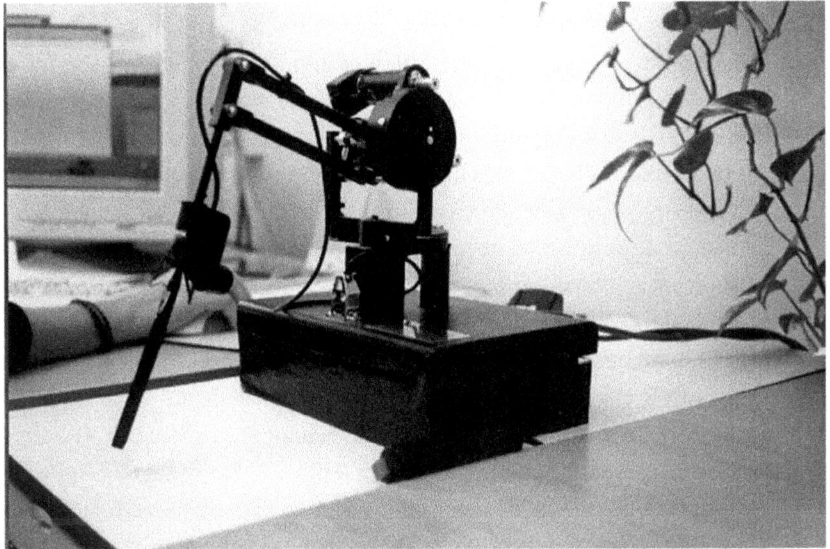

Figure 4 The PHANToM (Personal HAptic iNTerface Mechanism) at CERTEC, University of Lund, Sweden, 2000. Author's photograph.

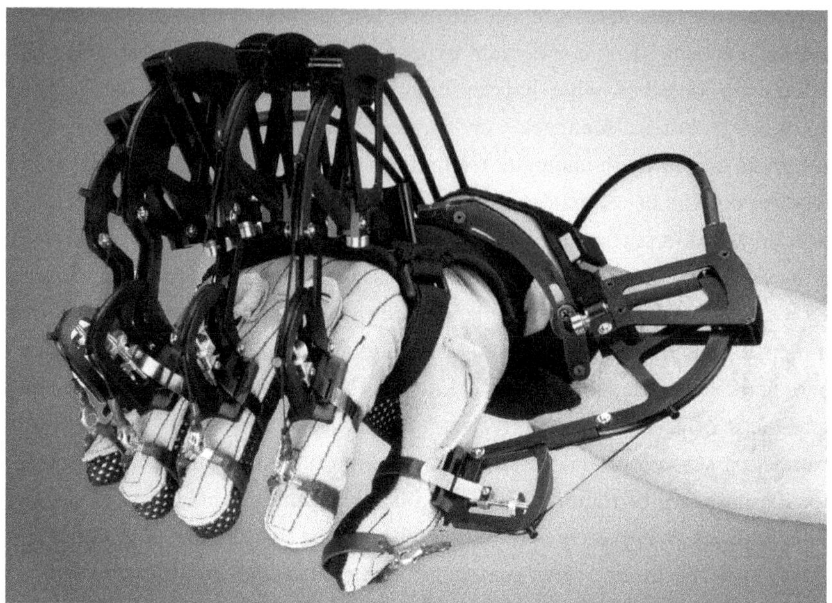

Figure 5 The CyberGrasp glove, from CyberGlove Systems LLC. **Source**: EST Engineering Systems Technologies GmbH & Co. KG, est-kl.com 2024.

From the user's perspective, then, the forms of touch that can be experienced can vary widely, ranging from precise sensations that replicate the surface texture of a three-dimensional virtual object (with the PHANToM, CyberGrasp, or more recent HaptX Gloves), or a real part of body anatomy during surgery (Da Vinci surgical robot), right down to a less precise locational vibration that supplements on-screen action in a videogame such as the sense of driving on rough ground or being hit by a bullet. Whether it is the more basic form of vibration, or the more advanced form of proprioceptive engagement with virtual objects, haptic feedback is often far more effective in combination with another modality such as the visual display of an object, or an audio notification. Indeed, the HaptX Gloves launched in 2023 are marketed precisely to users of Virtual Reality who can see and reach out for realistic-looking objects in stereoscopic 3D, but with the standard issue VR controllers cannot touch or manipulate them.

The long and fascinating history of haptic technologies since the ARM has been extensively documented elsewhere (e.g. Hillis, 1999; Iwata, 2008; Parisi, 2018; Paterson, 2007), but it is important to note that there is a functional divide between devices. Whereas the more advanced haptic devices are designed and engineered like the ARM to provide feedback to the human operator in order to perform sophisticated tasks, such as manipulating real or virtual objects in three-dimensional space, more basic haptics uses a small embedded motor to provide vibration against the skin or 'rumble' in the hands, and this serves as an extra communicative channel alongside, or in some cases instead of, visual display. Incorporating basic haptics in mobile devices has opened up an instantly recognizable and continuous haptic channel for communication. Of course, vibration as basic haptics has been present within mobile phones since Motorola's StarTAC in 1993, was subsequently adopted in mainstream 'dumb-phones' and is present within every smartphone around the world. Now that smartwatches are becoming a mainstream product category, the 'buzz' of smartphone notifications in one's hand or pocket can now be felt as timed vibrations on the skin of the wrist. This includes notifications of incoming email, texts, the proximity of Uber vehicles, a stream of map directions and much else besides. Such ubiquitous haptic messaging systems, Parisi argues, 'treat the skinspace of the wrist as an always-on communication channel that can be used for the transmission of coded messages, effectively establishing a material link between the wearer of the device and global flows of data' (2018, p. 329). In fact, a veritable explosion of professional-industrial and consumer haptics occurred in the 1990s which put haptics on the engineering map and made them mainstream and commercially successful. Still one of the most advanced haptic interfaces in existence, the PHANToM was designed at MIT in 1996 and was adopted for a range of purposes including industrial design and 3D modelling, and variations of its basic design are still commercially available. In-car controllers also discovered haptics, with BMW's iDrive system demonstrated in 1999 and integrated into their 7 Series in 2001. The holy grail for in-car touchscreen display is a screen with haptics, that offers the tactile illusion of a button press, something that Immersion Corporation is working on.

Perhaps the most rapid and successful adoption in the consumer space, however, has been videogame haptics, since their first appearance as vibration from motors embedded in the controller and felt in the player's hands. Since its first appearance as so-called 'rumble' within the add-on Rumble Pak for Nintendo's N64 controller in 1997, and the 'DualShock' controller for the original PlayStation that same year, haptics has been present within every successive generation of videogame controller for each multimillion-selling Sony PlayStation, Microsoft Xbox, and Nintendo console. From generation to generation the haptic content becomes more precise and higher-definition through a combination of hardware (motors) and software (drivers, and commands available to game developers through the Application Programming Interface or API). For example, the 'DualShock' rumble was built into successive generations of Sony consoles before Immersion Corporation helped co-develop the 'DualSense' controller with Sony for their PlayStation 5, released in 2020, which also includes haptic resistance in the controller's triggers. This mainstream haptics is not just felt in the hands. Commercially available haptics can also involve the forehead (Sony's PSVR2 virtual reality headset, released 2023), the upper body (Teslasuit, released 2017), and as noted, the skin of the wrist ('Taptic Engine' first in the Apple Watch from 2014, then iPhones from 2015).

The key to a convincing haptic interaction with a real or virtual object is the lack of latency, so that the manipulation of the object is 'felt' by the user in a way that corresponds immediately with actions performed on the screen. This is the case whether it is low-level 'rumble', more high-definition haptics in the controller or more advanced three-dimensional interaction with virtual objects. In terms of the neurophysiological narrative so far, haptic interfaces are feeding in to forms of 'discriminative' touch which predominantly employ the myelinated Aβ nerve fibres, as the rapidity of 'what' and 'where' information is important for sensing, grasping, and manipulating real and virtual objects in real time. Haptic interfaces provide stimuli for the discriminative touch system of the user through cutaneous pressure and, in their more advanced form, proprioception (force feedback). Human-machine interactions, which include Human-Computer Interaction (HCI) and Human Robot Interaction (HRI) in fact, have usually addressed only those forms of touching and proprioception necessary for the user to accomplish particular tasks. Of course, the full complexity of embodied touch, including its affective content, is not usually addressed by these engineering and commercial concerns.

Although we noted that haptics has routinely been used as an additional communicative channel, in terms of mainstream adoption, this usually means a 'buzz' or 'burr' to accompany an app-driven sonic notification. What about communicating social touch using haptic technologies, perhaps involving the CT afferents alongside the Aβ fibres through slow stroking behaviours? Although not a serious challenge to mainstream commercial haptics, there has nonetheless been a healthy diversity of projects which have tried to engage in affective or social touch through technologies, and which have sometimes questioned the very notion of what a haptic interface is. Before representative examples of such projects are detailed, we should acknowledge that the relationship between the 'medium' of haptic communication and the actual 'message' in McLuhan's terms (McLuhan, 1964) is not straightforward here. In human-computer interaction (HCI) and computer-mediated communication (CMC) research, for the most part, the interest in the engineering of haptic force-feedback interfaces such as the PHANToM and the CyberGrasp glove which form the 'medium' have ignored those studies in nonverbal communication, that is, the actual 'message'. But apart from accomplishing a task remotely with another operator, can affective content be expressed through such devices, and if so, how? Those studies on interpersonal touch and nonverbal communication discussed in Section 1.3 (Burgoon, 1991; Crusco & Wetzel, 1984; Fisher et al., 1976; Jones & Yarbrough, 1985) were ground-breaking at the time, but scholars who revisit that literature now find them lacking in depth and repeatability. There seem to be few studies which update or extend those findings in more recent social settings, although Margaret McLaughlin and her co-authors have, however, relied on such work, including Coker and Burgoon (1987), to explore how the 'immediacy' of presence and an agent's 'expressiveness' is communicated through the interface (McLaughlin et al., 2008, p. 160). Meanwhile, human–robot interaction (HRI) researchers are rediscovering the nonverbal communication literature to understand more about gesture and expressivity (see Section 2.2).

At MIT TouchLab, working with its Director Hiroshi Ishii and others, Angela Chang came up with ComTouch in 2002 as a Masters project on remote digital social touch. ComTouch offered a vision of a handheld vibrotactile device to augment remote audio-visual communication in real-time. The design was ergonomically modelled around a grasping hand, with places for the fingers to rest, squeeze or feel vibration. Unlike a conventional mobile phone, however, Chang's prototype had no screen, and the touch communication was bidirectional and synchronous. What is particularly impressive about this project, several years before smartphones became ubiquitous, is that the role of touch in nonverbal communication was central, and the guiding metaphor for the design concept was a haptic greeting: 'The concept of this handheld device was inspired by the communication metaphor of shaking hands – a nonverbal interaction where the information is characterized by the physical nature of the participants' (Chang, 2002, p. 27). Audio speakers were repurposed as vibrotactile devices, and placed tactically on the device under the fingers and fingertips, spaced out through trial and error. A series of experiments were then conducted with the device where users were tasked with negotiating a series of decisions together using both audio and tactile channels simultaneously, and the results showed the potential for a series of 'tactile gestures' that emerged between users (Chang, 2002, p. 54ff). ComTouch is therefore evidence of an early experiment in digital social touch through which nonverbal gestures were built into the project, and where users' own nonverbal communication was allowed to emerge naturalistically. Since its debut, the following two decades have brought up a number of similar small-scale design and engineering projects that prioritise the social and nonverbal aspects of touch.

Most commercially available haptic devices discussed so far, including the TeslaSuit and HaptX Gloves, address touch from a technoscientific and therefore physiological perspective. Against this, Carey Jewitt and Sara Price compel us to consider the social aspect of digital touch: 'We argue for moving beyond the replication of lived experiences of touch, to move beyond 'touch as a technoscience' to 'touch as a social sensory experience' that opens a door to new forms of touch and immersion' (Jewitt & Price, 2024, p. 30). Much of their recent book *Digital Touch* revolves around examples and vignettes of technologies that provide social touch, and even includes a 'Manifesto for digital social touch in crisis' as a conclusion. Moving away from the commercially available haptic devices discussed so far, they survey an ecosystem of smaller design-led devices for remote communication in the vein of ComTouch, some of which they employ as case studies in their InTouch project based at UCL. As they write, digital touch devices can serve as notification, for promoting awareness of another, or to 'foster physical intimacy between known/loved others, and/or support emotional well-being' (Jewitt & Price, 2024, p. 31), including easing anxiety and loneliness. They discuss a range of experiments that have proliferated in the wake of ComTouch to deliver touch sensations remotely, from mobile phones to communicate patterns of touch through vibrotactile actuators to the wearer's clothing (e.g. Huggy Pajama, Hugme), to gloves that provide thermal feedback (e.g. HotMits), or rings or wristbands that offer vibration to the finger or wrist (e.g. Ring!U). Unlike the commercially available techno-scientific solutions, such projects explicitly aim to deliver more emotive forms communication. For example, the Hey Bracelet (2022) is a commercially available device worn on the wrist and works in conjunction with a mobile phone app, and its manufacturer Feelhey promises 'you can send a touch to each other and receive a gentle squeeze in return' to another person's wrist (Feelhey.com, 2024). Jewitt and Price use this device as the basis for a vignette in the book that examines its use by two (fictional) geographically separated lovers. Although it can express a squeeze of short duration, a major disadvantage is that it is unsuited to more prolonged tactile engagement like hand-holding or stroking. With this device and a number of other comparable devices like haptic rings with biosensors that emerged during the pandemic lockdowns and thereafter, any touch communications are 'not easily editable or personalisable by users', meaning that it is difficult to achieve truly 'nuanced' tactile interaction, they argue (Jewitt & Price, 2024, p. 31). Furthermore, not all such devices allow reciprocity. The Hug Pillow, 'a pillow which responds through vibration and change in temperature to give a warm, comfortable, and soft sensation of a physical hug' (Jewitt & Price, 2024, p. 105), allows only one-way interaction, for example, while the Hey Bracelet only has asynchronous bi-directional interaction.

This section began with the ARM and the engineering desire of a fully rendered haptic simulation. Like the uncanny valley of anthropomorphism in robot design (Mori et al., 2012), in which anything that stops short of realistic human resemblance will instead look to our eyes as weird or strange, what makes digital touch seem realistic becomes limited by arbitrary factors. Experiencing a tactile interaction with the original high-end PHANToM device during doctoral research in 2000 (Paterson, 2023b), I was immediately impressed by the convincing sensations of metallic smoothness that were modelled for my fingertip through a stylus while simultaneously my eyes were seeing a visual render onscreen. However, move the stylus outside of its designated area, and the device suddenly goes loose and limp. The tactile illusion is shattered. Some of the less expensive examples show an inventiveness in finding alternative ways to achieve remote social touch, including generating sensations that are more indexical or symbolic rather than strictly representative of our physical experiences of touch, where the 'message' or meaning takes over from the 'medium'. With several of these devices including ComTouch and the Hey Ring, a particular vibrotactile pattern comes to stand for a nonverbal touch interaction, say a hug, but other factors including context, the duration and intensity of the vibration, and so on can alter the meaning of the nonverbal tactile communication. One of the case studies that Jewitt and Price designed and built for their InTouch project is what they call a Tactile Emoticon (Price et al., 2022), which became another vignette in their book. It is 'a system consisting of two paired mitts that enables two people to communicate remotely through tactile messages' (Jewitt & Price, 2024, p. 83). It beautifully illustrates how some of the limitations of engineering 'realistic' touch including vibrotactile and temperature factors can be overcome by relying on a deepening knowledge of personal contexts, as distinct and recognizable 'tactile biographies' come into play in effective digital touch communication:

> The Tactile Emoticon device enables pairs of people to communicate remotely by sending and receiving tactile messages by configuring vibration, pressure, and temperature. The couples using the device consistently drew on their knowledge of one another's touch practices and preferences and spoke of the importance of understanding one another's 'tactile biographies', 'touch signatures' or 'tactile identities' in the work of creating and interpreting tactile messages. This knowledge was used to enable them to configure the digital touch properties available to create nuanced and meaningful touch messages. (Jewitt & Price, 2024, p. 60)

Just one year before the first transatlantic 'handshake' between MIT and UCL that opened this section, the Zeus surgical robot grabbed headlines in 2001 as a robot-assisted remote laparoscopic cholecystectomy was conducted between New York and Strasbourg. Over the past decade or so, such telesurgery is becoming more routine, and the Da Vinci room-sized surgical robot is entrusted to perform more operations in more medical facilities. The manufacturer of the Da Vinci system claims more than 10 million operations have been performed (Intuitive.com 2024), and last year a video of a Da Vinci operation at Edward Hospital in Naperville, Illinois, sewing up a grape's delicate flesh with astonishing precision went viral on social media. As the surgeon peers intently into the large, hooded display and operates the console's controls, the actual robot arms operate smoothly and make small, incredibly precise movements. This is Goertz's ARM once again, the master/slave manipulation paradigm. Although the surgeon is conducting the operation in the same room, other Da Vinci robots have been operated from a large distance. The origins of robotic surgery include teleoperated systems developed by Stanford Research Institute (SRI) and then DARPA, with the intention to perform 'damage control surgery' and prevent trauma onsite rather than evacuate to field hospitals (George et al., 2018). Subsequent experiments involved using virtual reality head mounted displays (HMD) to provide telepresence for surgeons, but successive surgical robots in the 1990s, from Leonardo to Mona to Da Vinci ultimately in 1997, stabilized in form to become consoles where the surgeon sits and operates via articulated metal arms that output indirectly to patient-side manipulators. This is the perfect segue from haptic interfaces and virtual handshakes with telepresence to human–robot interactions and robot hugs in a space of proximity, perhaps.

2.2 Social Touch in Human-Robot Interaction (HRI): A Robot Hug

How might the neuroscientific discoveries outlined in Section 1 around 'social' or 'affective' touch be incorporated into human–robot interaction design? How might these forms of touch affect the movements and gestures of robot arms and hands, the use of an artificial touch layer or e-skin, and even the size and shape of the robot? Further, what potential is there for using robotic platforms as experimental laboratories to investigate the futures of affective touching more generally? Questions of touch and affect are now regarded as 'frontier topics' in human–robot interaction (Andreasson et al., 2017; Ventre-Dominey et al., 2019), and are regarded by some as essential for the design of social robots (e.g. Okamura, 2018), that is, autonomous or semi-autonomous robots that face the public and are designed for interaction as opposed to industrial robots which perform preprogrammed tasks. 'Tactile interaction is at the heart of human–robot relationships', as Walker and Bartneck (2013, p. 807) baldly state in their paper on receiving massage from robots. As Jung and Hinds (2018) observe, however, much of the social interaction with social robots remains within the laboratory rather than in more complex social settings 'in the wild' (2:1ff). Technologies such as artificial hands and e-skin are developing rapidly, and robots are increasingly targeted to domestic and healthcare tasks in proximity with human users. It is now opportune to ask about the role of social touch within human-machine interactions, and their role in what some roboticists are starting to call Artificial Empathy (AE), alongside the obvious requirements for Artificial Intelligence (AI). For example, papers by Minori Asada (Asada, 2015a, 2015b), and Paul Dumouchel and Luisa Damiano's work including their book *Living with Robots* (Dumouchel & Damiano, 2017). My contention in this section is not just to clarify the place of haptics within human–robot interaction, although various examples of robots that give or receive touch are provided. Rather, the point is to underline the significance of the role of touch and other forms of nonverbal communication in interactions with social robots, socially assistive robots and also service robots in healthcare and education settings. 'Socially assistive robotics' (SAR) is a distinct subset of social robots designed to train human users, and for those on the autism spectrum, those with dementia, or those with movement disorders who need forms of physical therapy, for example, socially assistive robots will increasingly be present in healthcare spaces, interacting with human users, but will need to earn their trust. Social touch, including haptic cues for guidance and the use of robot arms for gesture and nonverbal expression, will be increasingly valuable in building and enhancing that trust. By examining recent case studies of social robots designed to interact with humans through touch, in other words, we obtain a glimpse of the futures of human–robot interaction. This section is predominantly about human–robot interaction (HRI) design, then, and here I ask: how is social touch being folded into the human-machine present, and how are sociotechnical imaginaries of social touching in robots being envisioned?

The underlying socio-technological imaginaries of affective or social touch have an uneven record in their actual execution, as was clear from the previous section. This carries through to human–robot interaction. Increasingly, some of the same technologies which help to produce a sense of presence at a distance are being oriented to more social activities and social care tasks. The absolute necessity yet variability of the types of physical touch involved in the care professions is underlined when we consider the sheer number of settings or contexts in healthcare, social care, and education where it applies. For example, in healthcare there is guidance of the movement and help with ablutions for elderly patients or those with dementia, the rotation of bed-bound patients to prevent bedsores; in education, the reassurance of infants after emotional upset or everyday minor injury; in health and social care, the firm insistence necessary when psychiatric patients refuse to take their medications. Some contexts call for firm touch and physical strength, whereas others call for gentle reassurance and, if permitted, hugs, strokes or pats. Given the insistence by governments in advanced industrial economies such as Japan and the United States on developing service robots as solutions for healthcare, how is haptics operating in robot platforms, and what types of touch are being incorporated into human–robot interaction design? How can such basic human care for another, manifested through a host of conscious and unconscious types of contact, be articulated through motors and actuators? There are a few potential pathways for such technological applications.

Consider one of the most basic forms of nonverbal communication between humans that involve touch: a hug. Teaching a small child how to give and receive hugs is one of the easiest and most rewarding experiences, yet as we get older and become more self-conscious we become aware of a haptic protocol. Some people become hug-averse, others like to 'bring it in' and hold one firmly, and there may even be patting on the back or shoulder involved. Here is a description of a hug by scientists who have no expertise in nonverbal communication, using Fairhurst, McGlone and Croy's model of affective touch interaction discussed in Section 1, and cast in highly neutral terms. A hug, according to them, is

> an interdependent process where the sender and the receiver are simultaneously sending and receiving messages. Whether greeting, comforting, or bidding someone farewell, the sender initiates an exchange by sending an affective signal through a vehicle [i.e. a human body], like a comforting caress, which activates CT afferent receptors, in these cases for example, in the densely CT innervated back. The affective signal is received and recognised by the receiver who perhaps sends a reciprocal signal back, by leaning into the shoulder or hugging back. This expression is then recognised by the original sender. (Fairhurst et al., 2022, p. 58)

Interestingly, although the transmission and receipt of affective touch in their model could be dyadic, that is, based solely on touch, it more commonly involves other prompts, gestures and sensory stimuli within the interpersonal communication process. As they put it, 'a sigh or a change in eye gaze are other forms of sensory feedback that close the loop' (2022, p. 58). These types of actions are elsewhere helpfully referred to as 'intra-hug gestures' (Block et al., 2023). However, if the 'multisensory contributions to social touch, that is the sight, sound and smell of the person touching us' are so significant, argue (Marshall & McGlone, 2020, p. 56), this may explain why 'laboratory experiments like those using a robot are not ecologically valid'. The daunting difficulty of engineering haptic interactions such as hugs, handshakes or gestures which seem unremarkable between human interactants should not be underestimated. Hugs and handshakes with robots are difficult problems for hardware and software alike. 'Accurately replicating a human hug is a difficult problem because it requires realtime adaptation to a wide variety of users, close physical contact, and quick, natural responses to intra-hug gestures performed by the user', as Block et al. (2023, p. 18:12) explain. The difficulty factor is not preventing some roboticists from attempting it. Furthermore, some HRI researchers have recently revisited some of the historic social scientific research on haptics and proxemics featured in 1.3, as both haptics and proxemics feature in nonverbal communication. Even within nonverbal communication studies, touch has historically been sidelined or subservient to other modalities and communication channels, especially the verbal (including extralinguistic phenomena) and the visual (including the perception of body language, gesture etc.).

As Arnold and Scheutz argue, 'a turn to the tactile is more than due' in human–robot interaction, as HRI must investigate 'the *experienced behavior or disposition of the robot*' through its physical presence, and therefore how it elicits certain actions or responses from the human user (2017, p. 82, their emphasis). This includes robot morphology, the design of the shape of the robot form as well as its physical gestures. As is the case with hugs or handshakes, even task-based interactions between human user and social robot that seem basic is in fact highly complex. The respected HRI researcher Allison Okamura identifies the issues clearly, underlining the fundamental difficulty of integrating haptics into more complex underlying nonverbal communication protocols, and the necessity of choosing the optimal modality for accuracy and efficiency. She regards work in this area as a heavily interdisciplinary undertaking: 'Understanding appropriate robot design for physical/haptic human–robot interaction, from the mechanical to the algorithmic, requires amalgamated knowledge from a variety of fields outside traditional engineering/computer science, such as biomechanics, psychology, and neuroscience' (2018, p. 6:2). HRI research has therefore begun to revisit the nonverbal communication literature more systematically, and a study by Arnold and Scheutz (2018) involved user evaluations of human–robot tactile interaction, and found that 'robot-initiated touch' has been found 'to improve receptions of social robots by their interactants' (2018, p. 353), albeit with some disparities based on the evaluator's gender. Some ethnographies of human–robot interactions have also focused on nonverbal communication and haptics (Barker & Jewitt, 2022; Chun & Knight, 2020). The fact that physical and emotional well-being rely on interpersonal, or as Okamura puts it, 'human-human touch', correspondingly entails that 'human–robot touch will be important for usability and acceptance of many kinds of robots' (Okamura, 2018, p. 6:3). One reason for the return to the observation of human-human haptics, or the role of social touch in communication that we saw in 1.3, is an instrumental one, then, whereby the interdisciplinary field of interaction design can foster more supposedly naturalistic interactions between humans and robots in order to instil trust and increase acceptance with human users. Another reason is more socially responsible, to foster prosocial behaviours amongst certain isolated or vulnerable human groups, and this is where socially assistive robotics (SAR) can help train and encourage users by using touch and motor mimicry to signal approachability, invite users into the proximal space of interaction and facilitate nonverbal communication alongside verbal exchanges with robots.

Despite this recent resurgence of interest in the possibilities of nonverbal communication described in Section 1.3, the more specific engagement with touch, gesture and proprioception, what is collectively recognized within nonverbal communication literature as 'haptics' or the 'haptic channel' (Hall & Knapp, 2009), seems especially ripe for further exploration. When Tamie Salter and colleagues wrote fifteen years ago that 'communicating through natural touch or physical contact is an area which has not yet been fully explored by robot developers' (2006, p. 128), it remains relatively true to this day. The intervening years have not offered an abundance of robot platforms which specifically address this, but there have been clusters of research on robotic touch using existing platforms in various parts of the world. For example, robotic skin which incorporates pressure sensors has long been of interest (Casteñada, 2001; Hammock et al., 2013; Miyashita et al., 2007). Miyashita et al. (2007) had proposed a method for their robotic agent Robovie-IISa to detect human positions and postures by using tactile sensor data when a user is interacting with its thick outer electronic skin. For this robot, a kind of postural map of the user is constructed by interpolating possible combinations of haptic interaction by means of a piezoelectric film layer sandwiched between layers of silicone and urethane foam, with groups of sensor elements distributed at various points of the robotic body (2007, p. 527). From information provided through these tactile sensors, it is possible to estimate position and posture, and changes in user movement are tracked through IR cameras distributed around the room. While promising, this method assumes that users find touching robotic skin inherently inviting, which is not always the case, and users tend to use their right hands more than their left in physically touching the robot, which skews the map of the user. In any case, as Salter and colleagues argue, most touch sensors are based on microswitches 'which are very different from biological touch or surface sensors, e.g. the skin' (Salter et al., 2006, p. 128). As we have seen in the neurobiology of touch in 1.1, human skin affords a combination of different speeds and pressures of interaction through multiple nerve pathways, including stroking, pinching, gentle touching, warmth and so on, each with different intentions and user experiences. Robots with e-skin like

Robovie-IISa can respond to, and themselves model, discriminative forms of touching involving location and duration. However, the necessity to lower the barrier of communication with robots, to achieve more fluid, trusting, and intuitive human–robot interaction for human users who may be unfamiliar with robot platforms, requires a different form of touch communication, more akin to social touch than discriminative touch. It is not enough to provide robot platforms with higher-fidelity e-skin so that patterns of touch stimuli can be computed faster. Instead, through both software (algorithms, machine learning) and hardware (e-skin, robot arms with degrees of freedom), this is about identifying affective touching behaviours and then potentially modelling them through the robot, although this will additionally involve far more advanced motoric protocols in interaction design than are currently available.

In the first decade of the twenty-first century, several robots explored affective touch, but for various practical reasons and concerns around safety these were often intentionally nonhumanoid, designed to invite touch without being threatening in appearance to users without previous robot experience. Prominent examples were Yohanan and MacLean's 'Haptic Creature' (Yohanan & MacLean, 2008, 2011), AIST's Paro the seal and Omron Corp's NeCoRo cat, all with artificial fur to encourage stroking. For such projects the inclusion of affective forms of a user's tactile interaction with the robot was a primary motivation. Of their lap-based, fur-ensconced, rabbit-like robot, Yohanan and MacLean explain: 'The main goal of the Haptic Creature project is to investigate the basis of affective touch in social situations; and longer-term, to explore applications in companionship and therapy where touch is known to be influential, sometimes in the form of human-animal interactions' (2009, p. 4158). Such zoomorphic robots can therefore piggyback on the longer history of the use of animals in therapy, where touch is the principal means for interaction, and which involves beneficial outcomes for both human and animal. Elsewhere, Yohanan and MacLean explain what this relationship between touch and affect means for the human user in their interaction with the 'creature': 'An important aspect of social interaction is *affect display* – the external manifestation of internal emotional state – as it helps to regulate and add significance to the interaction' (2008, emphasis added). Yet, as Arnold and Scheutz (2017, 2018) argue, such affect display may be problematic for the area of robotics known as soft robotics which, through the use of softer external materials, positively invite tactile interaction and proximity. Aiming for automatic attributions of interiority or empathy through the use of materials and zoomorphic design, as is clearly the case with the Haptic Creature, Paro and NeCoRo, affords different types of touch interaction from human users than in any hard-bodied or android equivalents. In other words, based on prior experiences with petting animals, users are more likely to stroke the artificial fur of a zoomorphic robot in a way that mimics affective touch. We only ever touch intimate human partners in that same way, so how can android robots encourage affective touch behaviours without explicitly sexualizing them, say? As Arnold and Scheutz say, 'soft robotics is not just a rough translation of actions defined by machine code but also an interface that could change what is expected and what is practically possible for that code to express in robotic action', they remind us (2017, p. 85). As a result, soft robotics is not only about 'more engaging and lifelike surfaces and forms' involving 'skin', 'fur' or 'bodies' but about how 'more effective, helpful interactions' (Arnold & Scheutz, 2017, p. 86) can be fostered. This is a more difficult issue in the design of android robots, encouraging more effective tactile interactions without the benefits of pet-like appearance.

An earlier instance of a zoomorphic robot designed for haptic interaction was the Huggable from Walter Dan Stiehl, Cynthia Breazeal and others at MIT (Stiehl et al., 2005, 2009), which takes the form of a Teddy Bear with full-body fur embedded with touch and temperature sensors as well as inertia sensors to measure tilt orientation, somewhat mapping the human haptic system discussed in Section 1. Like the Haptic Creature, the Huggable's main purpose was therapy. Since the Huggable can only respond to touching intentions and behaviours rather than doing any touching itself, its design is effectively single purpose, inviting the touch of a user for potentially therapeutic purposes. Beneath the layer of fur is silicone skin designed to provide the right feel for the user, 'soft and "fleshy" like a creature, not hard like the traditional robot' (Stiehl et al., 2005, p. 4). Since so much interaction between humans and animals involves forms of touching, then, the Huggable design features a 'sensitive skin' with the possibility for detecting 'light touching' such as gentle stroking. This encourages the user to interact haptically. While trials were conducted elsewhere using Paro, AIBO and NeCoRo, they lacked the '*full body* sense of touch capable of properly detecting the affective content of touch', argued Stiehl and colleagues (2005, p. 1, original emphasis). Evaluating the Huggable in a paediatric care environment, elsewhere the team describe it as 'a full body, multi-modal sensitive skin system capable of detecting affective and social touch' (Stiehl et al., 2009, p. 318). Through the network of touch sensors, along with electric field sensors and QTC (force) sensors, the presence and proximity of a human user, and the detection of their hand's touching activities, can be determined by means of processing the combined information. Furthermore, since the temperature sensors required more prolonged contact than the other sensors, circa five seconds, 'this information is useful in cases such as squeezing, or hugging in which there is a long period of contact, such as through holding' (Stiehl et al., 2005, p. 5). This combination of sensors, including electric field sensors for user proximity detection and temperature sensors to detect various touching styles, together offer a demonstration that more complex affective touching behaviours can be interpreted. A study of the Huggable in a Boston paediatric hospital demonstrated how social robots 'could assist pediatric inpatients with critical and/or chronic health conditions who experience high levels of stress and pain' (Logan et al., 2019, p. 2). Not only did the child patients report a statistically significant higher positive affect (using PANAS-C self-report survey method) after interacting with Huggable but also self-reporting by the attending Child Life Specialists (CLS) showed they valued the opportunity to connect to their child patients in novel ways. Whereas emotional support and pain management is usually provided by medical staff, another benefit supported by the data was that parents reported lower levels of their children's pain (Logan et al., 2019, p. 6), with the implication that social robots like Huggable support the findings discussed by Field in Section 1.3 about the analgesic qualities of affective touch, in that 'interpersonal interaction with a trusted ally can mitigate perceptions of physical pain and increase comfort' (Logan et al., 2019, p. 7).

This prompts us to consider the broader social role of touch in socially assistive robotics (SAR), and its capacity to promote prosocial behaviours. As two of the pioneering researchers in this field, David Feil-Seifer and Maja Matarić, argue: 'SAR systems may be useful not just for their direct therapeutic applications but more generally as catalysts for social interaction' (2011, p. 25). For those isolated in elderly care homes, and without access to animal companions, a robot companion that encourages pro-social behaviours through touching and stroking is one answer. Paro the robot seal has sensors for light, touch, sound, temperature and posture, and can respond to touch and stroking through moving its head, opening and closing its eyelids, and making appropriate animal sounds. It has been used in care homes in its native Japan, Denmark, the Netherlands and the United States, and a study of psychogeriatric care in the Netherlands involving different levels of dementia showed enhanced interactions between residents, uplift in mood and enhanced functional self-care using the COOP/WONCA assessment amongst ninety-one participants (Bemelmans et al., 2015). Similarly, research on robots as autism therapy tools often report 'increased engagement, increased levels of attention, and novel social behaviours such as joint attention and spontaneous imitation when robots are part of the interaction'; and while some of these behaviours 'can be attributed to the fact that robots provide novel sensory stimuli', other behaviours 'such as turn-taking with another child, manifestations of empathy, or initiation of physical contact with the experimenter [. . .] suggest that robots occupy a special niche between inanimate toys (which do not elicit novel social behaviors) and animate social beings (which can be a source of confusion and distress to children with autism)', as Scassellati, Admoni and Matarić (2012, p. 276) found.

So far in this section on human–robot interaction the robot examples have invited affective touch, being zoomorphic and having soft surface textures that encourage stroking, hugging, and squeezing by human users. Teddy bears even without servomotors and sensor arrays afford such basic haptic interaction. This would be an opportune moment to revisit and build upon the research on nonverbal communication and interpersonal touch (Section 1.3) specifically in the context of recent human–robot interaction research. Such research has revealed for example that users who had interactions with specifically pet-like shapes showed improved vital signs such as lowered pain, anxiety, and blood pressure, as summarized by Hoffman and Krämer. This should come as no surprise, since it clearly echoes the effects observed from therapies with living animals. Previous research in this area, for instance, demonstrated that touching Paro, a soft robotic seal covered with fur, lowers depression, stress, and pain, 'effects that are also a common result of therapies with living animals' (Hoffmann & Krämer, 2021, p. 5). Moreover, other studies revealed that touch from a robot that possesses body parts that allow for touch, for example, arms, hands or grippers, evokes similar reactions to interpersonal touch (Hoffmann & Krämer, 2021, pp. 1–2). What of android robots designed to do the touching and hugging instead? A study by Bevan and Fraser (2015) for example revealed that a mediated handshake can increase cooperation during a negotiation task, compared to no handshake. Cramer, Kemper, Amin, Wielinga and Evers showed that Robosapien V2, a toy-like humanoid robot, was evaluated as more reliable and less machine-like by observers if the interaction included touch as opposed to no touch (Cramer et al., 2009).

Meanwhile, Hoffman and Krämer's 'The persuasive power of robot touch' does return to the classic nonverbal communication literature on touch in order to further it through the context of human–robot interaction. Human users were recruited to interact with a Softbank NAO robot, humanoid in form but rather small, and their study involved what they term 'robot-initiated' but 'non-functional touch'; that is, the robot either touched the left hand of the participant during the interaction, or did not touch the participant at all as a control state. When touch was initiated it was without any instrumental purpose, and therefore could be interpreted as an affective gesture. In a nutshell, their study 'focuses on the question whether non-functional [i.e. affective] robot-initiated touch can elicit positive behavioral and evaluative consequences in actual human–robot encounters, similar to the effects observed in the interpersonal context' (Hoffmann & Krämer, 2021, p. 8). The interactions were observed and filmed, and the results are quite eye-opening and unpredictable. First, in fifty-five out of ninety-six possible instances, participants reacted by smiling or laughing during or shortly after robot-initiated touch. Second, there was a statistical uptick in compliance, as 'participants who were touched were indeed more likely to comply [. . .] than participants who were not touched' (Hoffmann & Krämer, 2021, p. 21). There were apparently no notable effects on pro-social behaviours, such as the participant offering to help afterwards, but perhaps this was a limitation of the design of the study. In line with prior cited studies on the effects of users touching zoomorphic robots, there were emotional reactions to being touched back: 'participants who were touched by the robot indicated that they felt better during the conversation and reported lower negative affect subsequently. This implies that robot-initiated touch indeed improved participants' emotional state in comparison to the same interaction without touch' (Hoffmann & Krämer, 2021, p. 23). One of the limitations of the design of the study is that, apart from self-reported measures, no brain imaging of users or blood samples were taken to track oxytocin or other hormone levels. It is possible, however, that the simple robot-initiated touch, in combination with speech, could be calming and therefore responsible for the self-reported increase in positive affect. The results do lend evidence to the fascinating social psychology approach formulated by Nass and Moon (2000), according to which technologies can trigger deeply ingrained 'social cues', such as attributing gender and ethnic categories to computers, to which we can of course add robots. Although Nass and Moon refer to these responses by users as 'mindless', in that they are automatic and 'overlearned' (Nass & Moon, 2000, p. 90) through culture, they explain this is not reducible to mere anthropomorphism, the attribution of human qualities to nonhuman objects, animals or artificial counterparts in general.

Before we consider a robot specifically designed to hug, an intriguing teleoperated robot designed to interact with and touch hospital patients is being trialled, an example which lies between mediated social touch and robotics. The Välkky robot is designed by Edinburgh-based Touchlab and was one of the finalists for the $10 m ANA Avatar X-Prize in 2022. This is an annual competition to establish a remote presence and accomplish tasks at a distance via a robot platform. Välkky is being evaluated with nurses and patients in a new high-tech hospital facility in Helsinki. The idea is to administer care to isolated and immunocompromised patients in separate wards, with the user, a specialist nurse, wearing a tactile bodysuit (Teslasuit) in another room, teleoperating the robot avatar to interact with a patient. Through the Teslasuit the nurse operator has basic haptic feedback around the upper body and arms when the robot interacts with objects or touches a patient. As someone on the evaluation team explained, problems with intermittent internet coverage and speed introduced latency and uncertainty in the movements of the robot, which broke the illusion of being embodied in another place (personal communication). The smoothness of operation is compromised, and the goal of gentle touch interactions breaks down. In addition, the appearance of the robot to the patient is as a mechanical platform, and it was difficult for patients to discern or 'see' the nurse operator behind it. Some form of facial affect display has been discussed, but the risk is that it heightens the uncanny nature of this robotic form. Despite rather mundane technological problems shattering the illusion of haptic teleoperation through robot avatars, the example of Välkky still demonstrates the practical need as well as the potential for social touch at a distance in such human–robot interactions.

HuggieBot, as its name implies, is specifically designed to achieve one specific user interaction. Unlike Välkky, which is an extension of the teleoperator's body and designed to achieve a number of nursing tasks, HuggieBot 1.0 was conceived as a Masters project in the wake of personal loss to provide comforting interactions for those distant from loved ones. HuggieBot 1.0 was developed initially by Alexis E. Block in 2016 in Katherine J. Kuchenbecker's lab at the Max Planck Institute for Intelligent Systems in Stuttgart. Block is now based at Case Western Reserve University in Cleveland with her Social and Physical Human Interaction (SaPHaRI) lab, testing version 4.0. The HuggieBot project's purpose is 'to *provide an embodied affective robot that can supplement human hugs in situations when requesting this form of comfort from others is difficult or impossible*' (Block et al., 2023, p. 18:12, original emphasis). In engineering terms, HuggieBot 1.0 started as a modified version of the existing vaguely anthropomorphic Willow Garage PR2 platform, with wheels at the base and articulated arms, and versions of PR2 have been programmed to fold towels or pick up objects from the floor, for example. HuggieBot 2.0, 3.0 and 4.0 moved away from the PR2 to become a fully integrated custom robotic platform designed, built, and programmed by Block. HuggieBot 2.0 began testing in 2020 and used visual and haptic perception to deliver adaptive hugging in a closed-loop system, initiating the hug with a vocal communication ('Can I have a hug, please?') (see Figure 6). HuggieBot 3.0 in 2022 added two six-degree-of-freedom Kinova JACO arms, 'being anthropomorphic, quiet, and safe' (2023, p. 18:11), as their movement is kept slow and can be overpowered by a human user. The custom head unit consists of a screen which shows animated faces, a speaker, and an Intel RealSense Depth Sensing Camera. The torso is a stainless steel height-adjustable frame with what Block calls HuggieChest, consisting of inflatable padding with pressure sensors and heatpads. With its more anthropomorphic JACO arms, HuggieBot 3.0 gained a crucial feature, the ability to autonomously detect, and reciprocate, 'intra-hugging gestures' through a probabilistic behaviour algorithm (see Figure 7). Once a human user is detected in

Figure 6 HuggieBot 3.0, photo courtesy of Alexis E. Block, at the Max Planck Institute for Intelligent Systems, Stuttgart.

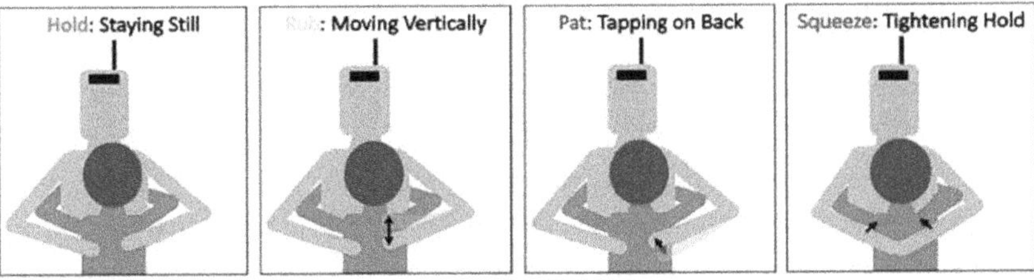

Figure 7 Diagram from Block et al. (2023, p. 18:13) showing the four 'intra-hug gestures' that HuggieBot 3.0 can perform, either in response to a user action or proactively when it does not detect any user actions.

the proximal space, HuggieBot 3.0 vocally communicates the intent to embrace ('I am ready for a hug'), displays a facial animation on its head-screen and positions its arms ready to slowly enclose the user. During the duration of the hug, users were instructed either to hold still, or to provide some haptic gestures like rubbing its back or squeezing it, and HuggieBot 3.0 provided some variety in response to the user in terms of gentle patterns of arm movement that equated to patting, rubbing, and squeezing. Over time, the preferences of users were logged and the authors were able to derive a 'probabilistic behavior model that determines which action the robot should perform based on which gesture it just detected from the user' (Block et al., 2023, p. 18:24). HuggieBot 4.0, in the early stages of designing and testing at the time of writing, adds the measurement of physiological responses, including oxytocin and cortisol levels, incorporates a social stress test into the study and further improves on the human–robot approach phase of the hug.

As explained previously, negotiating intra-hug gestures even between humans is a complex interpersonal and spatial calculus, and the team initially assumed that HuggieBot should simply mirror the human user's intra-hug gesture. However, results from their action-response elicitation study unexpectedly showed that straightforward mirroring was not evaluated so positively by the user. In post-hug interviews, users explained they appreciate variety in robot responses, that unpredictability 'leads users to feel it is more "alive"', and that straightforward mirroring felt 'too mechanical' (Block et al., 2023, p. 18:16). Instead, the modestly spontaneous robot hugging behaviour enabled by their 'simple probabilistic behaviour paradigm' succeeded in blending user preferences with spontaneity 'to reasonably match natural human exchanges of intra-hug gestures' (2023, p. 18:37). Combining variations of biomimicry and anthropomorphic behaviours in this way based on user testing seems to run counter to some nonverbal communication research findings between humans, where behavioural mimicry is an important component in social learning and can be used for the nonconscious persuasion of others (Roegiers et al., 2022; van Swol, 2003). However, in terms of the human-human protocols involved in greeting and communicating trust and affect, such as handshakes and hugs, some variation is expected.

As has been shown in this section, handshakes and hugs can involve socially complex haptic and proxemic calculations between humans, and are significant engineering challenges for any future human–robot interaction. As Block explained to me, HuggieBot was initially conceived to provide solace in the wake of personal loss, with waitlists for grief counselling compounding the fact that loved ones are often geographically distant (Interview, 03.06.24). When countenancing grief or other complex emotions, Block saw the necessity of social touch for fostering empathy, and the potential for this to be fulfilled by a robot. Many workers are long-distance commuters or spend significant amounts of time away from family for work. For submariners or astronauts, there is the additional factor of delayed communication environments, and the deep space missions that are realistically on the horizon will exacerbate the sense of isolation. In addition, for other groups such as children and adults with neurodiverse conditions such as autism and dementia, such non-threatening forms of artificial social touch can be encouraging and therapeutic: 'People working with children or in therapy are beginning to recognize that natural touch is an important form of interaction or communication with a robot', say Salter et al. (2007, p. 105), and proprioceptive and thermoreceptive properties are significant components within such 'natural' touch or interaction, as successive iterations of HuggieBot clearly show.

Social psychology research on biomimicry in recent decades, however, offers intriguing avenues for the link between nonverbal communication and HRI. As Chartrand and Lakin note, 'the mimicry of gross and fine motor movements (e.g., gestures, mannerisms, finger movements), facial expressions, and vocalizations is often nonconscious, unintentional, and effortless' (Chartrand & Lakin, 2013, p. 287). Elsewhere, Chartrand and Bargh discovered the 'chameleon effect' in which human subjects unconsciously and passively mimic the gestures and facial expressions of an interaction partner within a social environment to match their type of social expression and level of extroversion (Chartrand & Bargh, 1999, p. 283), and van Baaren et al. found 'increased prosocial orientation' for those mimicked, the hypothesis being that 'by increasing empathy, liking, and rapport, [mimicry] plays an important role in social interactions' (van Baaren et al., 2004, p. 71). Such findings would suggest the centrality of behavioural mimicry in Socially Assistive Robots such as the University of Glasgow and Herriott-Watt University's SoCoRo (Socially Competent Robot) project, whose robot Alyx employs a range of facial expressions and the use of hand gestures in interactions with users on the autism spectrum for behavioural learning training (BLT) (McKenna et al., 2018). By modelling various nonverbal expressions, the idea goes, SoCoRo can effectively train users to recognize and also enact important social cues in workplace interactions, for example. For HuggieBot, similarly, the invitation to hug must counter an initial wariness or hesitancy for human subjects, especially those with limited prior exposure to robots. Given this initial disposition of wariness or distrust of the robot in the human user, therefore, simply mirroring the gross motor movements of the user may not elicit prosocial effects by themselves, but it is the variations through intra-hug gestures that can help establish rapport and sustain enthusiasm by participants in the interaction, as Block et al. (2023) found.

Building upon what was observed previously by Okamura (2018) and others, therefore, the difficulty of establishing haptic and proxemic protocols in human–robot interactions offers real challenges for interaction design. Nevertheless, returning to, and building upon, the nonverbal communication literature seems a promising direction to help analyse this complex spatio-haptic negotiation. This, combined with the direct ethnographic observation of haptic interactions, may offer some of the necessary insights in human–robot interaction design for robotics teams, but also allow us to consider other robotic platforms as testbeds for experimenting with the role of touch in prosocial behaviours more generally. The haptics and proxemics observed in even relatively unsophisticated forms of human-human (interpersonal) interaction such as hand-shaking or hugs, as we have seen, is deceptively difficult to engineer in human–robot interaction. The richly complex social phenomenon of touching is unlikely to be effectively simulated in the near term, say McLaughlin et al., 'owing to the complexity of the other senses involved including the pliancy of tissue, the scent and warmth of the other, and the large scale of the simulation area' (2008, p. 173). However, from the Haptic Creature to the Huggable, and finally HuggieBot, this section has summarized some projects which are beginning to engage with the slower, more 'affective' touch that involves CT-afferents, even if the true complexity of 'social touch' is further over the horizon for human–robot interaction. There is no doubt that, eventually, robot-initiated touch can potentially unlock some of the rich neurophysiological responses we have seen (e.g. Field, 2001, 2014), plugging in to our deeply embedded social and developmental practices of touching, potentially widening the appeal of robots to diverse users.

References

Ackerley, R., Wasling, H. B., Liljencrantz, J., et al. (2014). Human C-tactile Afferents Are Tuned to the Temperature of a Skin-Stroking Caress. *The Journal of Neuroscience*, *34*(8), 2879–2883. https://doi.org/10.1523/jneurosci.2847-13.2014.

Adrian, E. D., & Zotterman, Y. (1926). The Impulses Produced by Sensory Nerve Endings. *The Journal of Physiology*, *61*(4), 465–483. https://doi.org/10.1113/jphysiol.1926.sp002308.

Ainsworth, M. D. S. (1979). Attachment as Related to Mother-Infant Interaction. In J. S. Rosenblatt, R. A. Hinde, C. Beer, & M.-C. Busnel (Eds.), *Advances in the Study of Behavior* (Vol. 9, pp. 1–51). Academic Press. https://doi.org/10.1016/S0065-3454(08)60032-7.

Andreasson, R., Alenljung, B., Billing, E., & Lowe, R. (2017). Affective Touch in Human–Robot Interaction: Conveying Emotion to the Nao Robot. *International Journal of Social Robotics*, *10*(4), 473–491. https://doi.org/10.1007/s12369-017-0446-3.

Arnold, T., & Scheutz, M. (2017). The Tactile Ethics of Soft Robotics: Designing Wisely for Human–Robot Interaction. *Soft Robotics*, *4*(2), 81–87. https://doi.org/10.1089/soro.2017.0032.

Arnold, T., & Scheutz, M. (2018). *Observing Robot Touch in Context: How Does Touch and Attitude Affect Perceptions of a Robot's Social Qualities?* Proceedings of the 2018 ACM/IEEE International Conference on Human-Robot Interaction, Chicago, IL, USA. https://doi.org/10.1145/3171221.3171263.

Arthur, C. (2002, Wednesday 30 October). Touching Moment 3,000 Miles Apart Becomes a Virtual Reality. *The Independent*, 7.

Asada, M. (2014). Towards Artificial Empathy. *International Journal of Social Robotics*, *7*(1), 19–33. https://doi.org/10.1007/s12369-014-0253-z.

Asada, M. (2015a). Development of Artificial Empathy. *Neuroscience Research*, *90*, 41–50. https://doi.org/10.1016/j.neures.2014.12.002.

Asada, M. (2015b). Towards Artificial Empathy: How Can Artificial Empathy Follow the Developmental Pathway of Natural Empathy? *International Journal of Social Robotics*, *7*(1), 19–33. https://doi.org/10.1007/s12369-014-0253-z.

Barker, N., & Jewitt, C. (2022). Filtering Touch: An Ethnography of Dirt, Danger, and Industrial Robots. *Journal of Contemporary Ethnography*, *51*(1), 103–130. https://doi.org/10.1177/08912416211026724.

Bastian, H. C. (1869). On the 'Muscular Sense', and on the Physiology of Thinking. *British Medical Journal*, *1*(435), 394–396. https://doi.org/10.1136/bmj.1.435.394.

BBC. (2002). *Lover's Touch Is Special*. http://news.bbc.co.uk/1/hi/health/2158489.stm.

Bemelmans, R., Gelderblom, G. J., Jonker, P., & de Witte, L. (2015). Effectiveness of Robot Paro in Intramural Psychogeriatric Care: A Multicenter Quasi-experimental Study. *Journal of the American Medical Directors Association*, *16*(11), 946–950. https://doi.org/10.1016/j.jamda.2015.05.007.

Bevan, C., & Fraser, D. S. (2015). *Shaking Hands and Cooperation in Tele-present Human-Robot Negotiation. Proceedings of the Tenth Annual ACM/IEEE International Conference on Human-Robot Interaction* (pp. 247–254), Portland, Oregon, USA. Association for Computing Machinery. https://doi.org/10.1145/2696454.2696490.

Block, A. E., Seifi, H., Hilliges, O., Gassert, R., & Kuchenbecker, K. J. (2023). In the Arms of a Robot: Designing Autonomous Hugging Robots with Intra-hug Gestures. *Transactions on Human-Robot Interaction*, *12*(2), 1–49. https://doi.org/10.1145/3526110.

Boddice, R., & Smith, M. (2020). *Emotion, Sense, Experience*. Cambridge University Press. https://doi.org/10.1017/9781108884952.

Burgoon, J. K. (1991). Relational Message Interpretations of Touch, Conversational Distance, and Posture. *Journal of Nonverbal Behavior*, *15*(4), 233–259. https://doi.org/10.1007/BF00986924.

Cannon, W. B. (1939). *The Wisdom of the Body*. W.W. Norton.

Casteñada, C. (2001). Robotic Skin: The Future of Touch? In S. Ahmed, & J. Stacey (Eds.), *Thinking Through the Skin* (pp. 223–236). Routledge.

Chang, A. (2002). *ComTouch: A Vibrotactile Mobile Communication Device*. MIT Press.

Chartrand, T. L., & Bargh, J. A. (1999). The Chameleon Effect: The Perception–Behavior Link and Social Interaction. *Journal of Personality and Social Psychology*, *76*(6), 893–910. https://doi.org/10.1037/0022-3514.76.6.893.

Chartrand, T. L., & Lakin, J. L. (2013). The Antecedents and Consequences of Human Behavioral Mimicry. *Annual Review of Psychology*, *64*, 285–308. https://doi.org/10.1146/annurev-psych-113011-143754.

Chun, B., & Knight, H. (2020). The Robot Makers: An Ethnography of Anthropomorphism at a Robotics Company. *ACM Transactions on Human-Robot Interaction*, *9*(3), 1–36. https://doi.org/10.1145/3377343.

Coker, D. A., & Burgoon, J. K. (1987). The Nature of Conversational Involvement and Nonverbal Encoding Patterns. *Human Communication Research*, *13*(4), 463–494. https://doi.org/10.1111/j.1468-2958.1987.tb00115.x.

Cole, J. (1995). *Pride and a Daily Marathon* (1st Ed.). MIT Press.

Craig, A. D. (2003). Interoception: The Sense of the Physiological Condition of the Body. *Current Opinion in Neurobiology, 13*(4), 500–505. https://doi.org/10.1016/s0959-4388(03)00090-4.

Cramer, H., Kemper, N., Amin, A., Wielinga, B., & Evers, V. (2009). 'Give Me a Hug': The Effects of Touch and Autonomy on People's Responses to Embodied Social Agents. *Computer Animation and Virtual Worlds, 20*(2–3), 437–445. https://doi.org/10.1002/cav.317.

Crusco, A. H., & Wetzel, C. G. (1984). The Midas Touch: The Effects of Interpersonal Touch on Restaurant Tipping. *Personality and Social Psychology Bulletin, 10*(4), 512–517. https://doi.org/10.1177/0146167284104003.

Dumouchel, P., & Damiano, L. (2017). *Living with Robots* (M. DeBevoise, Trans.). Harvard University Press.

Ebbinghaus, H. (1902). *Grundzüge der psychologie*. Veit.

Ellingsen, D. M., Leknes, S., Loseth, G., Wessberg, J., & Olausson, H. (2015). The Neurobiology Shaping Affective Touch: Expectation, Motivation, and Meaning in the Multisensory Context. *Frontiers in Psychology, 6*, Article 1986. https://doi.org/10.3389/fpsyg.2015.01986.

Erlanger, J., & Gasser, H. S. (1930). The Action Potential in Fibers of Slow Conduction in Spinal Roots and Somatic Nerves. *American Journal of Physiology, 92*(1), 43–82. https://doi.org/10.1152/ajplegacy.1930.92.1.43.

Fairhurst, M. T., McGlone, F., & Croy, I. (2022). Affective Touch: A Communication Channel for Social Exchange. *Current Opinion in Behavioral Sciences, 43*, 54–61. https://doi.org/10.1016/j.cobeha.2021.07.007.

Fechner, G. T. (1860). *Elemente der Psychophysik*. von Breitkopf und Härtel.

Feil-Seifer, D., & Mataric, M. (2011). Socially Assistive Robotics. *IEEE Robotics & Automation Magazine, 18*(1), 24–31. https://doi.org/10.1109/mra.2010.940150.

Field, T. (2001). *Touch*. MIT Press.

Field, T. (2014). *Touch* (2nd Ed.). MIT Press.

Field, T., Hernandez-Reif, M., Diego, M., Schanberg, S., & Kuhn, C. (2005). Cortisol Decreases and Seratonin and Dopamine Increase Following Massage Therapy. *International Journal of Neuroscience, 115*(10), 1397–1413. https://doi.org/10.1080/00207450590956459.

Field, T. M., Schanberg, S. M., Scafidi, F., et al. (1986). Tactile/Kinesthetic Stimulation Effects on Preterm Neonates. *Pediatrics, 77*(5), 654–658. https://doi.org/10.1542/peds.77.5.654.

Fisher, J. D., Rytting, M., & Heslin, R. (1976). Hands Touching Hands: Affective and Evaluative Effects of an Interpersonal Touch. *Sociometry, 39*(4), 416–421. https://doi.org/10.2307/3033506.

Foerster, O. (1936). The Motor Cortex in Man in the Light of Hughling Jackson's Doctrines. *Brain*, *59*(2), 135–159. https://doi.org/10.1093/brain/59.2.135.

Foerster, O., & Gagel, O. (1932). *Die Vorderseitenstrangdurchschneidung beim Menschen*. Julius Springer.

Fretwell, E. (2020). *Sensory Experiments: Psychophysics, Race, and the Aesthetics of Feeling*. Duke University Press. www.dukeupress.edu/sensory-experiments.

George, E. I., Brand, T. C., LaPorta, A., Marescaux, J., & Satava, R. M. (2018). Origins of Robotic Surgery: From Skepticism to Standard of Care. *Jsls*, *22*(4). https://doi.org/10.4293/jsls.2018.00039.

Gibson, J. J. (Ed.). (1968). *The Senses Considered as Perceptual Systems*. George Allan & Unwin.

Haans, A., & Ijsselsteijn, W. (2006). Mediated Social Touch: A Review of Current Research and Future Directions. *Virtual Reality*, *9*(2), 149–159. https://doi.org/10.1007/s10055-005-0014-2.

Haans, A., & Ijsselsteijn, W. (2009). The Virtual Midas Touch: Helping Behavior after a Mediated Social Touch. *IEEE Transactions on Haptics*, *2*(3), 136–140. https://doi.org/10.1109/TOH.2009.20.

Haggarty, C. J., Malinowski, P., McGlone, F. P., & Walker, S. C. (2020). Autistic Traits Modulate Cortical Responses to Affective but Not Discriminative Touch. *European Journal of Neuroscience*, *51*(8), 1844–1855. https://doi.org/10.1111/ejn.14637.

Hall, J. A., & Knapp, M. L. (2009). *Nonverbal Communication in Human Interaction* (7th Ed.). Cengage Learning. https://doi.org/10.1515/9783110238150.

Hammock, M. L., Chortos, A., Tee, B. C.-K., Tok, J. B.-H., & Bao, Z. (2013). 25th Anniversary Article: The Evolution of Electronic Skin (E-Skin): A Brief History, Design Considerations, and Recent Progress. *Advanced Materials*, *25*(42), 5997–6038. https://doi.org/10.1002/adma.201302240.

Harlow, H. F. (1958). The Nature of Love. *American Psychologist*, *13*(12), 673–685. https://doi.org/10.1037/h0047884.

Heslin, R., & Alper, T. (1982). Touch: A Bonding Gesture. In J. M. Wiemann & R. P. Harrison (Eds.), *Nonverbal Interaction* (pp. 47–75). Sage.

Hillis, K. (Ed.). (1999). *Digital Sensations: Space, Identity and Embodiment in Virtual Reality*. University Of Minnesota Press.

Hoffmann, L., & Krämer, N. C. (2021). The Persuasive Power of Robot Touch. Behavioral and Evaluative Consequences of Non-functional Touch from a Robot. *PLoS One*, *16*(5), e0249554. https://doi.org/10.1371/journal.pone.0249554.

Howes, D. (2009). *The Sixth Sense Reader*. Berg.

Huisman, G. (2012). A touch of affect: Mediated social touch and affect. *Proceedings of the 14th ACM International Conference on Multimodal Interaction*, Santa Monica, CA. https://doi.org/10.1145/2388676.2388746.

Huisman, G. (2017). Social Touch Technology: A Survey of Haptic Technology for Social Touch. *IEEE Transactions on Haptics*, *10*(3), 391–408. https://doi.org/10.1109/TOH.2017.2650221.

Iggo, A. (1960). Cutaneous Mechanoreceptors with Afferent C Fibres. *The Journal of Physiology*, *152*(2), 337–353. https://doi.org/10.1113/jphysiol.1960.sp006491.

Iriuchijima, J., & Zotterman, Y. (1960). The Specificity of Afferent Cutaneous C Fibres in Mammals. *Acta Physiologica Scandinavica*, *49*(2–3), 267–278. https://doi.org/10.1111/j.1748-1716.1960.tb01952.x.

Iwata, H. (2008). History of Haptic Interface. In M. Grunwald (Ed.), *Human Haptic Perception: Basics and Applications* (pp. 355–361). Birkhäuser Basel. https://doi.org/10.1007/978-3-7643-7612-3_29.

James, W. (1890). *The Principles of Psychology*. H. Holt and Company

Jeannerod, M. (1985). *The Brain Machine: The Development of Neurophysiological Thought* (D. Urion, Trans.). Harvard University Press.

Jewitt, C., & Price, S. (2024). *Digital Touch*. Polity Press. https://books.google.com/books?id=BxYLEQAAQBAJ.

Johansson, R. S., Trulsson, M., Olsson, K. Å., & Westberg, K. G. (1988). Mechanoreceptor Activity from the Human Face and Oral Mucosa. *Experimental Brain Research*, *72*(1), 204–208. https://doi.org/10.1007/BF00248518.

Jones, S. E., & Yarbrough, A. E. (1985). A Naturalistic Study of the Meanings of Touch. *Communication Monographs*, *52*(1), 19–56. https://doi.org/10.1080/03637758509376094.

Jung, M. & Hinds, P. (2018). Robots in the Wild: A Time for More Robust Theories of Human-Robot Interaction. *ACM Transactions on Human-Robot Interaction*, *7*(1), 1–5.

Katz, D. (1989). *The World of Touch* (L. E. Krueger, Ed.). Lawrence Erlbaum. https://books.google.co.uk/books?id=49Vtnp2k1MEC.

Kim, J., Kim, H., Tay, B. K., et al. (2004). Transatlantic Touch: A Study of Haptic Collaboration over Long Distance. *Presence*, *13*(3), 328–337. https://doi.org/10.1162/1054746041422370.

Kumazawa, T., & Perl, E. R. (1977). Primate Cutaneous Sensory Units with Unmyelinated (C) Afferent Fibers. *Journal of Neurophysiology*, *40*(6), 1325–1338. https://doi.org/10.1152/jn.1977.40.6.1325.

Logan, D. E., Breazeal, C., Goodwin, M. S., et al. (2019). Social Robots for Hospitalized Children. *Pediatrics*, *144*(1), e20181511. https://doi.org/10.1542/peds.2018-1511.

Lombroso, C. (1876). *L'Uomo delinquente*. Bocca.

Marshall, A. G., & McGlone, F. P. (2020). Affective Touch: The Enigmatic Spinal Pathway of the C-tactile Afferent. *Neuroscience Insights*, *15*, 2633105520925072. https://doi.org/10.1177/2633105520925072.

McGlone, F., Wessberg, J., & Olausson, H. (2014). Discriminative and Affective Touch: Sensing and Feeling. *Neuron*, *82*(4), 737–755. https://doi.org/10.1016/j.neuron.2014.05.001.

McGlone, F. P., & Walker, S. C. (2020). 4.06– The Neurobiological Basis of Affective Touch. In B. Fritzsch (Ed.), *The Senses: A Comprehensive Reference* (2nd Ed.) (pp. 67–78). Elsevier. https://doi.org/10.1016/B978-0-12-809324-5.24227-2.

McKenna, P. E., Ghosh, A., Aylett, R., Broz, F., & Rajendran, G. (2018). Cultural Social Signal Interplay with an Expressive Robot. IVA '18. *International Conference on Intelligent Virtual Agents* (211–218). Association for Computing Machinery.

McLaughlin, M., Jung, Y., Peng, W., Jin, S., & Zhu, W. (2008). Touch in Computer-Mediated Communication. In E. A. Konijn, S. Utz, M. Tanis, & S. B. Barnes (Eds.), *Mediated Interpersonal Communication* (pp. 158–176). Routledge.

McLuhan, M. (1964). *Understanding Media: The Extensions of Man* (1st Ed.). McGraw-Hill.

Merleau-Ponty, M. (2013). *Phenomenology of Perception* (D. Landes, Trans.). Taylor & Francis. https://books.google.co.uk/books?id=Lh_e0_y1YjgC.

Miyashita, T., Tajika, T., Ishiguro, H., Kogure, K., & Hagita, N. (2007). Haptic Communication between Humans and Robots. In S. Thrun, R. Brooks, & H. Durrant-Whyte (Eds.), *Robotics Research: Springer Tracts in Advanced Robotics* (pp. 525–536). Springer .

Montagu, A. (1971). *Touching: The Human Significance of the Skin*. Columbia University Press.

Montagu, A. (Ed.). (1986). *Touching: The Human Significance of the Skin* (3rd Ed.). Harper and Row.

Mori, M., MacDorman, K. F., & Kageki, N. (2012). The Uncanny Valley. *IEEE Robotics & Automation Magazine*, *19*(2), 98–100. https://spectrum.ieee.org/the-uncanny-valley (M. Mori, 'The Uncanny Valley', Energy, *7*(4), 33–35, 1970 (in Japanese)).

Morrison, I. (2016a). Affective and Social Touch. In J. D. Greene, I. Morrison, & M. E. P. Seligman (Eds.), *Positive Neuroscience* (pp. 7–20). Oxford University Press. https://doi.org/10.1093/acprof:oso/9780199977925.003.0002.

Morrison, I. (2016b). Keep Calm and Cuddle on: Social Touch as a Stress Buffer. *Adaptive Human Behavior and Physiology*, *2*(4), 344–362. https://doi.org/10.1007/s40750-016-0052-x.

Morrison, I. (2023). Touching to Connect, Explore, and Explain: How the Human Brain Makes Social Touch Meaningful. *The Senses and Society*, *18* (2), 92–109. https://doi.org/10.1080/17458927.2023.2200065.

Morrison, I., Loken, L. S., & Olausson, H. (2010). The Skin as a Social Organ. *Experimental Brain Research*, *204*(3), 305–314. https://doi.org/10.1007/s00221-009-2007-y.

Nass, C., & Moon, Y. (2000). Machines and Mindlessness: Social Responses to Computers. *Journal of Social Issues*, *56*(1), 81–103. https://doi.org/10.1111/0022-4537.00153.

Nordin, M. (1990). Low-Threshold Mechanoreceptive and Nociceptive Units with Unmyelinated (C) Fibres in the Human Supraorbital Nerve. *The Journal of Physiology*, *426*, 229–240. https://doi.org/10.1113/jphysiol.1990.sp018135.

Okamura, A. M. (2018). Haptic Dimensions of Human-Robot Interaction. *ACM Transactions on Human-Robot Interaction*, *7*(1), 1–3. https://doi.org/10.1145/3209768.

Olausson, H., Lamarre, Y., Backlund, H., et al. (2002). Unmyelinated Tactile Afferents Signal Touch and Project to Insular Cortex. *Nature Neuroscience*, *5*(9), 900–904. https://doi.org/10.1038/nn896.

Olausson, H., Wessberg, J., Morrison, I., McGlone, F., & Vallbo, A. (2010). The Neurophysiology of Unmyelinated Tactile Afferents. *Neuroscience Biobehavioral Reviews*, *34*(2), 185–191. https://doi.org/10.1016/j.neubiorev.2008.09.011.

Olausson, H. W., Cole, J., Vallbo, A., et al. (2008). Unmyelinated Tactile Afferents Have Opposite Effects on Insular and Somatosensory Cortical Processing. *Neuroscience Letters*, *436*(2), 128–132. https://doi.org/10.1016/j.neulet.2008.03.015.

Parisi, D. (2018). *Archaeologies of Touch: Interfacing with Haptics from Electricity to Computing*. University of Minnesota Press.

Paterson, M. (2006). Feel the Presence: Technologies of Touch and Distance. *Environment and Planning D: Society and Space*, *24*(5), 691–708. https://doi.org/10.1068/d394t.

Paterson, M. (2007). *The Senses of Touch: Haptics, Affects, and Technologies*. Routledge.

Paterson, M. (2009). Haptic Geographies: Ethnography, Haptic Knowledges and Sensuous Dispositions. *Progress in Human Geography*, *33*(6), 766–788. https://doi.org/10.1177/0309132509103155.

Paterson, M. (2019). On Pain as a Distinct Sensation: Mapping Intensities, Affects, and Difference in 'Interior States'. *Body and Society*, *25*(3), 100–135. https://doi.org/10.1177/1357034x19834631.

Paterson, M. (2021). *How We Became Sensorimotor: Movement, Measurement, Sensation*. University of Minnesota Press.

Paterson, M. (2023a). Fatigue as a Physiological Problem: Experiments in the Observation and Quantification of Movement and Industrial Labor, 1873–1947. *History and Technology*, *39*(1), 65–90. https://doi.org/10.1080/07341512.2023.2226288.

Paterson, M. (2023b). Getting a Grip on New Objects, Technologies, and Sensations through Aura, Presence, and Mimesis. In P. Vannini (Ed.), *The Routledge International Handbook of Sensory Ethnography* (pp. 53–68). Routledge.

Perl, E. R. (1971). Is Pain a Specific Sensation? *Journal of Psychiatric Research*, *8*(3), 273–287. https://doi.org/10.1016/0022-3956(71)90024-0.

Price, S., Bianchi-Berthouze, N., Jewitt, C., et al. (2022). The Making of Meaning through Dyadic Haptic Affective Touch. *ACM Transactions in Computer-Human Interaction*, *29*(3), 1–42, Article 21. https://doi.org/10.1145/3490494.

Raisamo, R., Salminen, K., Rantala, J., Farooq, A., & Ziat, M. (2022). Interpersonal Haptic Communication: Review and Directions for the Future. *International Journal of Human-Computer Studies*, *166*, 102881. https://doi.org/10.1016/j.ijhcs.2022.102881.

Robles-De-La-Torre, G. (2006). The Importance of the Sense of Touch in Virtual and Real Environments. *IEEE Multimedia*, *13*(3), 24–30. https://doi.org/10.1109/MMUL.2006.69.

Roegiers, S., Corneillie, E., Lievens, F., et al. (2022). Distinctive Features of Nonverbal Behavior and Mimicry in Application Interviews through Data Analysis and Machine Learning. *Machine Learning with Applications*, *9*, 100318. https://doi.org/10.1016/j.mlwa.2022.100318.

Salter, T., Dautenhahn, K., & Boekhorst, R. T. (2006). Learning about Natural Human–Robot Interaction Styles. *Robotics and Autonomous Systems*, *54*(2), 127–134. https://doi.org/10.1016/j.robot.2005.09.022.

Salter, T., Michaud, F., Létourneau, D., Lee, D. C., & Werry, I. P. (2007). Using Proprioceptive Sensors for Categorizing Human-Robot Interactions. *Proceeding of the ACM/IEEE International Conference* (105–112). Association for Computing Machinery.

Scassellati, B., Admoni, H., & Matarić, M. (2012). Robots for Use in Autism Research. *Annual Review of Biomedical Engineering*, *14*(1), 275–294. https://doi.org/10.1146/annurev-bioeng-071811-150036.

Schirmer, A., Croy, I., & Ackerley, R. (2023). What Are C-tactile Afferents and How Do They Relate to 'Affective Touch'? *Neuroscience & Biobehavioral Reviews*, *151*, 105236. https://doi.org/10.1016/j.neubiorev.2023.105236.

Sheridan, T. B. (1989). Telerobotics. *Automatica*, *25*(4), 487–507. https://doi.org/10.1016/0005-1098(89)90093-9.

Sherrington, C. S. (1906). *The Integrative Action of the Nervous System*. C. Scribner's Sons.

Sherrington, C. S. (1907). On the Proprio-ceptive System, Especially in Its Reflex Aspect. *Brain*, *29*(4), 467–482. https://doi.org/10.1093/brain/29.4.467.

Sterling, P., & Eyer, J. (1990). Allostasis: A New Paradigm to Explain Arousal Pathology. *Handbook on Life Stress, Cognition, and Health*, 629–649.

Stiehl, W. D., Lee, J. K., Breazeal, C., et al. (2009). The Huggable: A Platform for Research in Robotic Companions for Pediatric Care. *Proceedings of the 8th International Conference on Interaction Design and Children* (pp. 317–320), Como, Italy. Association for Computing Machinery. https://doi.org/10.1145/1551788.1551872.

Stiehl, W. D., Lieberman, J., Breazeal, C., et al. (2005). Design of a Therapeutic Robotic Companion for Relational, Affective Touch. ROMAN 2005. IEEE International Workshop on Robot and Human Interactive Communication, 2005.

Thayer, S. (1986). History and Strategies of Research on Social Touch. *Journal of Nonverbal Behavior*, *10*(1), 12–28. https://doi.org/10.1007/BF00987202.

Titchener, E. B. (1908). The Tridimensional Theory of Feeling. *The American Journal of Psychology*, *19*(2), 213–231. https://doi.org/10.2307/1412760.

Tsetserukou, D., Neviarouskaya, A., Prendinger, H., Kawakami, N., & Tachi, S. (2009, 10–12 September 2009). Affective Haptics in Emotional Communication. *2009 3rd International Conference on Affective Computing and Intelligent Interaction and Workshops* (pp. 1–6), Amsterdam, Netherlands.

Vallbo, Å., Olausson, H., Wessberg, J., & Norrsell, U. (1993). A System of Unmyelinated Afferents for Innocuous Mechanoreception in the Human Skin. *Brain Research*, *628*(1), 301–304. https://doi.org/10.1016/0006-8993(93)90968-S.

Vallbo, Å. B. (2018). Microneurography: How It Started and How It Works. *Journal of Neurophysiology*, *120*(3), 1415–1427. https://doi.org/10.1152/jn.00933.2017.

Vallbo, Å. B., & Hagbarth, K. E. (1968). Activity from Skin Mechanoreceptors Recorded Percutaneously in Awake Human Subjects. *Experimental Neurology*, *21*(3), 270–289. https://doi.org/10.1016/0014-4886(68)90041-1.

Vallbo, A. B., Olausson, H., & Wessberg, J. (2009). Pleasant Touch. In L. R. Squire (Ed.), *Encyclopedia of Neuroscience* (pp. 741–748). Academic Press. https://doi.org/10.1016/B978-008045046-9.01916-1.

Vallbo, Å. B., Olausson, H., & Wessberg, J. (1999). Unmyelinated Afferents Constitute a Second System Coding Tactile Stimuli of the Human Hairy Skin. *Journal of Neurophysiology, 81*(6), 2753–2763. https://doi.org/10.1152/jn.1999.81.6.2753.

van Baaren, R. B., Holland, R. W., Kawakami, K., & van Knippenberg, A. (2004). Mimicry and Prosocial Behavior. *Psychological Science, 15*(1), 71–74. https://doi.org/10.1111/j.0963-7214.2004.01501012.x.

van Swol, L. M. (2003). The Effects of Nonverbal Mirroring on Perceived Persuasiveness, Agreement with an Imitator, and Reciprocity in a Group Discussion. *Communication Research, 30*(4), 461–480. https://doi.org/10.1177/0093650203253318.

Ventre-Dominey, J., Gibert, G., Bosse-Platiere, M., et al. (2019). Embodiment into a Robot Increases Its Acceptability. *Scientific Reports, 9*(1), 10083. https://doi.org/10.1038/s41598-019-46528-7.

Walker, R., & Bartneck, C. (2013, 26–29 August 2013). The Pleasure of Receiving a Head Massage from a Robot. 2013 IEEE RO-MAN.

Weber, E. H. (1996). *E.H. Weber on the Tactile Senses* H. E. Ross, & D. J. Murray (Eds.), (2nd Ed.). Taylor & Francis.

Wessberg, J., Olausson, H., Fernstrom, K. W., & Vallbo, A. B. (2003). Receptive Field Properties of Unmyelinated Tactile Afferents in the Human Skin. *Journal of Neurophysiology, 89*(3), 1567–1575. https://doi.org/10.1152/jn.00256.2002.

Wundt, W. M. (1896). *Grundriss der Psychologie*. W. Engelmann.

Yohanan, S., & MacLean, K. E. (2008). The Haptic Creature Project: Social Human-Robot Interaction through Affective Touch. *Proceedings of the AISB 2008 Symposium on the Reign of Catz & Dogs: The Second AISB Symposium on the Role of Virtual Creatures in a Computerised Society* (pp. 7–11). The Society for the Study of Artificial Intelligence and Simulation of Behaviour,

Yohanan, S., & MacLean, K. E. (2009). A Tool to Study Affective Touch CHI '09 Extended Abstracts on Human Factors in Computing Systems, Boston, MA, USA. https://doi-org.pitt.idm.oclc.org/10.1145/1520340.1520632.

Yohanan, S., & MacLean, K. E. (2011). The Role of Affective Touch in Human-Robot Interaction: Human Intent and Expectations in Touching the Haptic Creature. *International Journal of Social Robotics, 4*(2), 163–180. https://doi.org/10.1007/s12369-011-0126-7.

York, G. K., III, & Steinberg, D. A. (2011). Hughlings Jackson's Neurological Ideas. *Brain, 134*(10), 3106–3113. https://doi.org/10.1093/brain/awr219.

Zotterman, Y. (1936). Specific Action Potentials in the Lingual Nerve of Cat. *Skandinavisches Archiv Für Physiologie*, *75*(3), 105–119. https://doi.org/10.1111/j.1748-1716.1936.tb01558.x.

Zotterman, Y. (1937). A Note on the Relation between Conduction Rate and Fibre Size in Mammalian Nerves 1. *Skandinavisches Archiv Für Physiologie*, *77*(2), 123–128. https://doi.org/10.1111/j.1748-1716.1937.tb01174.x.

Zotterman, Y. (1939a). The Nervous Mechanism of Touch and Pain. *Acta Psychiatrica Scandinavica*, *14*(1–2), 91–97. https://doi.org/10.1111/j.1600-0447.1939.tb06617.x.

Zotterman, Y. (1939b). Touch, Pain and Tickling: An Electro-Physiological Investigation on Cutaneous Sensory Nerves. *The Journal of Physiology*, *95*(1), 1–28. https://doi.org/10.1113/jphysiol.1939.sp003707.

Zotterman, Y. (1979). How It Started: A Personal Review. In D. R. Kenshalo (Ed.), *SensoryFunctions of the Skin of Humans* (pp. 5–22). Springer. https://doi.org/10.1007/978-1-4613-3039-4_2.

Cambridge Elements

Histories of Emotions and the Senses

About the Series

Born of the emotional and sensory "turns", Elements in Histories of Emotions and the Senses move one of the fastest-growing interdisciplinary fields forward. The series is aimed at scholars across the humanities, social sciences, and life sciences, embracing insights from a diverse range of disciplines, from neuroscience to art history and economics. Chronologically and regionally broad, encompassing global, transnational, and deep history, it concerns such topics as affect theory, intersensoriality, embodiment, human–animal relations, and distributed cognition. The founding editor of the series was Jan Plamper.

Cambridge Elements

Histories of Emotions and the Senses

Elements in the Series

Making Noise in the Modern Hospital
Victoria Bates

Academic Emotions: Feeling the Institution
Katie Barclay

Sensory Perception, History and Geology: The Afterlife of Molyneux's Question in British, American and Australian Landscape Painting and Cultural Thought
Richard Read

Love in Contemporary Technoculture
Ania Malinowska

Memes, History and Emotional Life
Katie Barclay and Leanne Downing

Boredom
Elena Carrera

Marketing Violence: The Affective Economy of Violent Imageries in the Dutch Republic
Frans-Willem Korsten, Inger Leemans, Cornelis van der Haven and Karel Vanhaesebrouck

Beyond Compassion: Gender and Humanitarian Action
Dolores Martín-Moruno

Uncertainty and Emotion in the 1900 Sydney Plague
Philippa Nicole Barr

Sensorium: Contextualizing the Senses and Cognition in History and Across Cultures
David Howes

Zionism: Emotions, Language, and Experience
Ofer Idels

Affective Touching: Neurobiology and Technological Applications
Mark Paterson

A full series listing is available at: www.cambridge.org/EHES

For EU product safety concerns, contact us at Calle de José Abascal, 56–1°, 28003 Madrid, Spain or eugpsr@cambridge.org.

www.ingramcontent.com/pod-product-compliance
Ingram Content Group UK Ltd.
Pitfield, Milton Keynes, MK11 3LW, UK
UKHW022144080726
473066UK00010B/744

* 9 7 8 1 0 0 9 4 8 4 3 7 4 *